Escaping Education

Studies in the
Postmodern Theory of Education

Joe L. Kincheloe and Shirley R. Steinberg
General Editors

Vol. 36

PETER LANG
New York • Washington, D.C./Baltimore • Boston
Bern • Frankfurt am Main • Berlin • Vienna • Paris

Madhu Suri Prakash
and Gustavo Esteva

Escaping Education

Living as Learning within Grassroots Cultures

PETER LANG
New York • Washington, D.C./Baltimore • Boston
Bern • Frankfurt am Main • Berlin • Vienna • Paris

Library of Congress Cataloging-in-Publication Data

Prakash, Madhu Suri.
Escaping education: living as learning within grassroots
cultures/ Madhu Suri Prakash and Gustavo Esteva.
p. cm. — (Counterpoints; vol. 36)
Includes bibliographical references and index.
1. Education—Philosophy. 2. Postmodernism and education. 3. Right to
education. 4. Multicultural education. I. Esteva, Gustavo. II. Title.
III. Series: Counterpoints (New York, N.Y.); vol. 36.
LB14.7.P73 370'.1—dc21 97-38841
ISBN 0-8204-3327-6
ISSN 1058-1634

Die Deutsche Bibliothek-CIP-Einheitsaufnahme

Prakash, Madhu Suri:
Escaping education: living as learning within grassroots cultures/ Madhu Suri
Prakash and Gustavo Esteva. –New York; Washington, D.C./Baltimore;
Boston; Bern; Frankfurt am Main; Berlin; Vienna; Paris: Lang.
(Counterpoints; Vol. 36)
ISBN 0-8204-3327-6

Cover design by Andy Ruggirello.

The paper in this book meets the guidelines for permanence and durability
of the Committee on Production Guidelines for Book Longevity
of the Council of Library Resources.

Printed in the United States of America.

Table of Contents

I am ashamed to think how easily we capitulate to badges and names, to large societies and dead institutions . . . I ought to go upright and vital, and speak the rude truth in all ways. If malice and vanity wear the coat of philanthropy, shall that pass?

Ralph Waldo Emerson, Self-Reliance

All rivers run to the sea;
yet the sea is not full;
unto the place from whence
the rivers come, thither
they return again.

Ecclesiates.

Go to the people. Live
among them. Learn from
them. Love them. Start
with what you know.
Build on what they have.
But of the best leaders
when their task is done,
the people will remark:
"We have done it ourselves."

Chinese Poem.

Prologue

O my soul, do not aspire to immortal life, but exhaust the limits of the possible.
Pindar, *Pythian* iii

Naming the intolerable is itself the hope.
John Berger, *And Our Faces, My Heart, Brief as Photos*

Radical hope is the essence of popular movements.
Douglas Lummis, *Radical Democracy*

This book takes the all-too-familiar tale of education and stands it on its head.

We do not tell the history of education from the perspective of the educated. We write about what we have learned to learn from those who have no access to education; who cannot get the developed person's prescribed quota or recipe for education; or those who, having trustfully and diligently undergone the education planned for them, have by now come to know too well the bitter taste of false expectations, dubious benefits, or failed promises.

This book does not attempt to package and sell one more reform initiative or proposal about improving or expanding the educational system. It has no new literacy project for the illiterate. It has no "informal education" remedy for those left sick or incapacitated by "formal education." It does not create multicultural medicines for the diseases of monoculturalism.

Instead, it celebrates well-being: still enjoyed in the commons and cultures of peoples living and learning at the grassroots. It celebrates the cultural richness, the prolific abundance that still exists in the many and diverse worlds of the social majorities. For they need no classrooms, no computer workshops, no laboratories nor libraries, nor even

Walmarts to teach and learn from each other. They have not forgotten their diverse arts of survival and flourishing "in lieu of education."

We write for our friends within the social majorities, courageously taking the initiatives we describe in our book. In telling their stories here, we hope that they will find further inspiration and arguments for their initiatives; for strengthening and carrying further their endeavors to protect their cultural spaces; to prevent the cultural meltdown of the global classroom.

We also write for our colleagues and friends in the educational system who share our concerns, our perplexities, our disenchantment, our frustrations with educational outcomes, our anguish with the horror of what the educated do to each other as well as to the uneducated and the illiterate.

We hope that we can be of some use in building strong walls to contain and limit the ambitions of the educational enterprise—today, as in the past, aspiring to save the world.

The social majorities need no saviors, no conscientization, no empowerment. They are impressively skillful in saving their worlds. They have been able to do so for five hundred years. The newly minted expert as well as the established scholar have much to learn about living well from the uneducated and the illiterate—if they can give up the arrogance of their expertise.

We suspect that many educators will find it difficult to follow our argument to the end, and that many others will resist or reject it from the very beginning—perceiving it as a threat to their expertise. We hope that those dismissing us will at least dare to give serious consideration to our insights and experiences—however counterfactual or counterintuitive these appear.

Educators who cannot bear to impose their universe of the academy upon the untamed pluriverse that still stretches beyond its boundaries will resonate with the ideas explored here. For those within the academy who sense its counterproductivity, the line of ideas followed here will not appear like paths to Nowhere: impractical, irrelevant, or utopian. Educators who cherish cultural diversity will find in these pages more reasons to curtail the spread of their own dis-ease, their plague.

Our encounters with the Other are no longer burdened by the Mission of saving their Minds, as our predecessors braved the world of savages and primitives to save their Souls. Freed from any and all salvational projects—of educators, developers, and others of their ilk—our journeys into the lands of the illiterate and the uneducated are filled with delightful surprises of discovering the riches of the Other, with the joy of the unknown and the unexpected that invariably constitute these adventures beyond education.

As pilgrims, we journey to places where notions of the good life have not been contaminated or destroyed by the plague of *Homo educandus* or *Homo oeconomicus*. We journey to gaze, to learn, to come to understand how magnificently they flourish in the absence of our needs, necessities, or certainties—jobs, day-care, classrooms, offices, eateries, restaurants, hospitals, and other constitutive elements of the global economy.

We would like to offer for consideration John Berger's (1991) observation: naming the intolerable is itself the hope. Naming the horror impels people to do something about it. All those who read these pages may not share the specific hope we have discovered among the social majorities. All the same, we hope that they will be less prone to impose their own salvational urges on the Other. We know that our arguments are unavoidably controversial. But nothing in these pages can be called a closed game. From this collection of seeds, many diverse fruits can be grown, eaten, and enjoyed.

Part I

Education as a Human Right:
The Trojan Horse of Recolonization

By old habit or new force, carrot or stick, educators and education are rapidly changing . . . to stay unchanged.

Blind political and economic forces are pushing the educational system out of the global market. To protect it in this turbulent time, educators, parents, governments, corporations, its guardians and consumers, continue to commit their will to the latest brands of educative potions and ever-new trinkets or teaching technologies.

The uneducated, the miseducated, and the undereducated are neither blind to, nor non-conscientized about, those efforts and processes. They are capable of seeing through the latest educational formulae being concocted for their secular salvation. They have their own ways, their own rich and ancient traditions for expressing their disenchantment, skepticism, or discontentment with the education they got or failed to get. They are teaching each other how to become refuseniks.

The counterproductivity of education and the educational system is evidenced in almost two centuries of history. The time has come to abandon this modern myth; not to give it a new lease on life with its postmodernization.

Enough is enough! ¡Ya basta!

* * *

What is good for the goose is good for the gander. In fact, education is a good for the goose precisely because it is good for the gander, according to assumptions and conclusions of the educated. It is a universal genderless *good*; so good, indeed, as to be declared a basic human *need*; so needed as to be claimed a universal human *right*.

One man's meat is another man's poison. Refuseniks are learning to resist any and all universal formulae of salvation; to recognize the cultural roots of each promoted globalism or universalism; to realize that all of them—including the different brands or breeds of education—are nothing but arrogant particularisms. What for some people is the proverbial dream come true, for other people is a waking nightmare: a plague, a disease destructive of their traditions, their cultural and natural spaces.

In the epic now evolving at the grassroots, the social majorities are taking steps to liberate themselves from the social minorities. Those classified and categorized as uneducated, underdeveloped, poor or undeveloped are struggling for their freedom from those who consider themselves to be educated or developed. Step by step, the former are dismantling all the institutions and projects of the latter which discriminate against them—including the educational enterprise.

In articulating these initiatives as "Grassroots Postmodernism," we seek lucidity, courage, and imagination. These are necessary for creating solidarities with communities and groups suffering the most marked and vicious discrimination of our times—imposed by the educated as professional assistance, aid, or help upon the three contemporary [lower] castes: the miseducated, the undereducated or the noneducated, who constitute the majority of people on earth, the Two-Thirds World.

The Different Faces and Facets of Education

Education is celebrated as a cherished gift by the educated. Singing songs in praise of it, they describe how it offers different freedoms: to realize personal dreams, visions, and careers; to open the mind; to live the good life; to bring about social justice and equality; to realize democracy—conventional, progressive, or radical; to celebrate one's own cultural inheritance; to enjoy and promote cultural diversity. . . .

What does this gift of education mean for the women and the men, the young and the old who constitute the social majorities of the world? those belonging to what are currently called "the cultures of silence"?

Freedom and Mobility for the Individual
Radical, liberal, and conservative educators promise social mobility for escaping marginalization—economic, political, or cultural. People

are educated to aspire for and approach the centers of power and control by their teachers, their liberators, their emancipators, their empowerers.

Mobility overcomes marginalization—goes the familiar global chant of education. Mobile individuals, like their cultures, escape the marginalization of people going Nowhere; of cultures stuck in their past; dwelling rather than pursuing progress by "moving and shaking."

Through their education, however, children learn to leave home, not to stay home. The psychological and cultural price of this impact cannot be measured (Berry 1990, 164). The new social norm implies that the child's destiny is not to succeed the parents, but to outmode them; succession is substituted for supercession. Neither school nor university looks toward passing on an unimpaired cultural inheritance. Instead, they push and promote the professional career. This orientation is "necessarily theoretical, speculative, and mercenary." The emphasis is on earning money in a provisional future that has nothing to do with place, commons, or community. Parents and children are separated from each other; made useless to one another (Berry 1990, 163).

In the worlds of the uneducated, in the cultures of dwelling, elders, parents, and neighbors teach and learn traditions which emphasize staying well rooted; strengthening the knowledge and skills needed to nourish and be nourished by their own places. Their ways of knowing, of living and learning, contain little or, better yet, *nothing* of the knowledge the educated need for their social mobility (Berry 1972, 1977, 1983, 1987, 1991a, 1991b; Prakash 1994).

The Indian peoples of Oaxaca in southern Mexico, to take one example, have flourished, as have their places, because of their traditions of teaching and learning. Their diverse cultures have continued to be enriched despite the abuses and interventions they have suffered from all kinds of Outsiders—ranging from the Aztecs in the pre-Hispanic world to national elites or transnational corporations in contemporary times.

Centuries upon centuries, they have been exposed to every variety of foreign imposition upon their lives and beliefs. Unlike indigenous peoples across the globe who have disappeared, died off, or been melted into the oblivion of the so-called national "melting pot," the sixteen Indian peoples of Oaxaca have successfully kept regenerating their language and culture, while coexisting with, as well as resisting, their colonizers' universalizable truths. Their evolving modes of cultural coexistence protect their pluriverse, adapting to each new condition of oppression and domination without losing their historical continuity. In recent years, they seem to be transforming their *resistance* into a *struggle of liberation*.

In four out of every five municipalities in the pluriverse of Oaxaca, differentiated moral and political traditions prevail, enriched through the intense interactions which these peoples have maintained over centuries with other cultures, whether dominant or dominated. They express neither the need nor desire for formal codes to give official definition to their traditions—well known and embraced by every member of the community. Their system of justice seeks neither the abstract impersonality nor the neutrality that supposedly defines the modern judicial system, being exported worldwide from the West.[1]

"Westerners," observed Marcos Sandoval of the Triqui people of Oaxaca, "represent justice with a blindfolded woman. We want her with her eyes well open, to fully appreciate what is happening. Instead of neutrality or impartiality, we want compassion. The person committing a crime needs to be understood, rather than submitted to a trial" (in conversation).

These open eyes of their justice do not, for example, look for punishment when a person violates a shared custom. He or she is perceived as someone in trouble who needs understanding and help, including the opportunity to offer compensations to the victim of his or her fault. If inadvertently, unintentionally, or because of a lack of prudence, someone burns a part of the forest, he or she must reforest it. If a man kills another, he must assume full responsibility for the welfare of the dead person's family for the rest of their lives. Rather than confine wrongdoers in jail, they seek to create experiences that encourage the doers of damage to calm down, to reflect on the violence of their crime, for a safe return from their delirious conditions. These practices are not conceived as forms of punishment. Instead, they offer communal support: according opportunities for the soul to heed the wisdom and advice of elders when they come to converse and reflect with those who have wronged others. Among peoples where these regimes of communal justice fully prevail, the incidence of all sorts of "crimes" or wrong doings is far lower than among the abstract citizens upon whom the State inflicts its legal regime, proclaiming the equality and impartiality of fair trials—one type of human right prized among many as a part of human "progress."

The Indian peoples of Oaxaca have been able to protect their indigenous regimes of justice against the threats of the Spanish Inquisition;

later, from the ferocity of the dictatorship in Mexico at the end of the nineteenth century; from the impulses of revolutionary governments in the first part of this century; and then again, from the modernizing fever of public developers who fell upon them during the last fifty years. In all these centuries of cultural resistance to "the Other," the Oaxaca Indians relied upon their own traditions; including the *tradition for changing their tradition*. This has helped them to adjust and enrich their regimes of justice, adapting them to every new condition. At the same time, it has helped them to hold on to the unique cultural leitmotivs of their traditions: themes that have kept them as peoples within their own original and unique cultural pluriverse.

Currently, however, all these differentiated cultural groups and small communities are confronting a new threat. Governmental as well as nongovernmental agencies and institutions are proselytizing another global morality implicit in the Universal Declaration of Human Rights. They persist in invading all communities with their "secular" religion of human rights.

"I can no longer do what is fair," reflects Rómulo Santiago, municipal president of Huayapam, near Oaxaca City; "every time I try to bring justice to our community, applying our traditional practices to amend wrongdoings, a human rights activist comes to stop me" (in conversation).

This contemporary threat has many faces. One face is that of establishing national and international juridical procedures that supersede communal customs for establishing fairness and justice. The other face is that of the gamut of "social rights" associated with economic development and progress.

To those struggling hard to maintain the autonomy of their cultures, human rights activists or agents of the government explain that all human beings must claim the universal human right to health, employment, modern medicine, sewage, roads, and other social services. They are urged to present their claims before the pertinent State authorities for obtaining whatever they "need." They are educated by the educated to conclude that education is undoubtedly among the most "basic" of human "needs"—the wrench of reason needed to open parochial, nonmodern minds to change and progress.

Give a man a fish, you feed him for one day. Teach a man to fish, you feed him for life. Better yet, educate a man for life, and you give him the wherewithal not only to similarly educate others for life, but to be able to discover all that he "needs," and must consequently claim as his Human Rights—Welfare as well as Liberty Rights.

Education is both a welfare and a liberty right. It promises security: of jobs, pensions, health care . . . These are the familiar strains of, by, and for education. They are sung to seduce peasants and other marginals into parting from their children; to gladly hand them over to the elementary doorkeepers of the Neoliberal Global Economy.

The carrots and sticks of seduction or fear distract the upward or outward bound from studying the underbelly of education. When studied from up close, we discover with others that those who become addicted to classroom instruction end up losing real opportunities for gaining the knowledge and skills with which communities endure and flourish; that the more their commons and communities are destroyed, the more dependent they become on diplomas; that the more diplomas are distributed, the more difficult it is to procure them; that while their procurement becomes a more difficult uphill enterprise, the economic value of credentials and diplomas slumps downhill—with rapidly reducing guarantees of access to salaried jobs; that the "lucky" few who wangle their way into acquiring job-guaranteed credentials form crippling dependencies upon salaries which come and go with the vagaries of international currency markets; that *the masses* must settle for minimum wages or unemployment minus welfare in the growing global economy.[2]

Professional Careers for Growth, Security and Satisfaction
Pride in the professions is justified by promises fulfilled: of personal growth, security, and satisfaction. Entrance to the professions must be deserved; won by the worthy; by dint of hard work; by honestly earned merit; with geese and gander alike lifting themselves up by their unisex bootstraps—free of the privileges of birth, caste, color, creed, or age.

To feed and foster the economy of the "disabling professions" (Illich & Kenneth 1977), education destroys the economy of home and community. These are left weak and vulnerable when people are no longer useful to one another. As this vulnerability grows, people fall into dependence on exterior economies and organizations. The local schools have no use for the local community; "they serve the government's economy and the economy's government" (Berry 1990, 164). Education for "community busting" establishes itself through "the hegemony of professionals and professionalism" (Berry 1990, 164).

Professionals are educated to "erect local failure." For educators and educated alike, "the locality exists merely as a market for consumer goods and as a source of 'raw material,' human and natural" (Berry 1990, 164). They learn to lose "pride in [their] surroundings";

to feel no poetry about the home life. The village scenes become "a sealed book." The local culture "is presented . . . as imbecile, barbarous, superstitious and useless for all practical purposes" (Gandhi 1953, 33). Saved from the parochial cultures of the *hillbilly,* the *ganwaar* (villager), the *red neck,* or the *local yokel,* education for the economy of professionals leaves "young people . . . contemptuous of the calling of their fathers." "Almost from the commencement, the text-books . . . never [teach the student] any pride in his surroundings . . . His education is calculated to wean him from his traditional . . . ancient culture . . ." (Gandhi 1946, 32–33).

Gandhi's truth (Gandhi 1946, 1970) refers not only to the education that the colonialists imposed upon their Third World colonies. Documenting how "the country becomes the colony of the city" in democracies like America today, Berry describes how "a vast amnesia invades the countryside"; how "local knowledge and local memory move away to the cities or are forgotten under the influence of homogenized sales talk, entertainment, and education" (Berry 1990, 156–157).

While a few benefit from the economy of professional careers, the many suffer the loss of "local knowledge and local memory." The professions ignore or write this off as "one of the cheaper prices of progress." Other careerists use this local failure to transform it into "the business of folklorists" (Berry 1990, 157).

Only those marginal to the educational enterprise or the economy of professional careers still sense that

> when community falls, so must fall all the things that only community life can engender and protect: the care of the old, the care . . . of children, family life, neighborly work, the handing down of memory . . . respect for nature and the lives of wild creatures (Berry 1990, 157).

Cultural Survival, Enrichment, and Diversity

Entrance into or advancement within the economy—national, international or global—is among the "lesser" (though necessary) functions served by education. Its higher function is cultural continuity, enrichment, and diversity.

Yet, wherever education advances, homogenization establishes itself. With every advancement of education or the educated, a "global monoculture spreads like an oil slick over the entire planet." The five thousand languages that currently survive can be seen as threatened species—in danger of extinction. Within a generation or two, not many of these languages will survive, if current trends continue. Of the languages that are alive today, only one percent survive in Europe and educated North America. It is scarcely an accident that "the home of literacy as well as the nation-state" has only one percent of the languages that survive (Sachs 1992, 102).

While languages are dying and disappearing, the academic industry for the mummification and preservation of "endangered tongues" continues to boom. Between 1950 and 1970, "about fifty languages have died each year; half of those still spoken in 1950 survive only as subjects for doctoral theses" (Illich 1977, 7).

The case of Mocho offers a glimpse of the typical pattern induced by the economy of education. Only seventy-five elderly speakers of Mocho remain in Chiapas, Mexico. With their death, Mocho will die. A few thousand miles north in Ohio, the academic industry for "preserving" this language is promoting multicultural education. Fifty years from now, the only records of Mocho will be found in an American university or some other haven of multicultural education.

The story of Mocho is the story of what happens when the children of a community, pursuing the promises of education, systematically learn to forget the languages of their commons and their communities. All it often takes are two generations of school-going offspring to send the language of their Elders up north to a corporate, State, or federally funded linguistic zoo.

While some members of the academy *preserve* Mocho in their archives and libraries (locked in the prison of space and time within dead leaves—the pages of the text or the book), other members are opening the doors of equal educational opportunity for the children of Mocho speakers. Education in the national language promises them access to the economy—unlike Mocho, which keeps them attached to their immobile culture and place. But, promises multicultural education, they can have their cake and eat it too. They can learn about Mocho history, language, and culture, while at the same time shaping up for being shipped out into the international economy; learning to clamber higher on the career ladder designed for the educationally able and competent; for those who want to do well in the One World, the Global Village.

The story of Mocho repeats itself wherever the educational system successfully enters, persists, and expands. In *every* corner of the world, cultural destruction and decimation follow as communities learn to *take-off* on the education runway. In Mexico, among the Triqui peoples of San Andrés Chicahuaxtla, Benjamín Maldonado discovers that the school is the road to ignorance of the local culture. On the education road, he observes that among the children and youngsters who currently attend school, 30 percent totally ignore their elders' indigenous knowledge of soil culture (agriculture), 60 percent acquire a dispersed and fragmented knowledge of it, while only 10 percent may be considered as capable of sustaining, regenerating and passing it on (Maldonado 1988).

Those who do not send their children down this road, however, keep alive and regenerate their cultures. Among the children and youngsters who do not attend school, 95 percent acquire the indigenous knowledge that defines and distinguishes their culture, while only 5 percent ignore it—those being children living outside the community for a long time. Sucking up the time, energy, and imaginative capacities of children with compulsory classroom attendance as well as homework, schools pose a terrible threat to the agrarian wisdom of the Triqui peoples. They impede the young from accompanying the adults of the community in their cultural practices, including those of working the soil, the *milpa*. To appreciate the ignorance imparted by the Western school within the soil cultures of the world, it is important to note that soil (*agri*) culture in Mexico, India, Guatemala, Peru, as well as in the other parts of the world, is not mere technical knowledge. There is a rich and complex set of rites and myths that give life to traditional agriculture; to make it a part of the living memory and imagination of the young of their communities; learning to sow by propitiating the land, the rain; learning to harvest by giving thanks to the forces of nature; learning how to avoid the impunities of scientific intervention; learning to respect the cycles of the moon or the wind; learning the relationships and places of people in the community; acquiring all the nuances and subtleties of their native languages . . . School promises "liberation" from these bonds of community and tradition: from what the professional educator has come to classify all over the world as "family exploitation" and "traditional superstition"— opposed to "true science."

Schools transform the children of the Triquis into cultural parasites. Educated children, Maldonado carefully documents, no longer know how to care for or contribute to the economy of the household and the community. Instead, they require money for learning to grow up; thus becoming cultural aliens in their own worlds. For the schooled Triqui, as for the schooled or educated Indians of other places and climes, "real life" lies outside the family and community. To help their children live this "real life," farming families must engage in the "sacrifice" needed to acquire the "superior" truths of science; and for making "advancements" in the economy.

The *real* price for education exacted and painfully extracted from the cultures of dwelling, Maldonado reveals, is the loss of language and culture. Falquet's (1995) studies describe in detail how Indian cultures are endangered or processed out of existence by the great acculturating educational machinery. Schools create a deep division, ripping apart the community, dividing it up into "the illiterates," who do not know the Latin alphabet because their knowledge is *only* oral, and the literates, who minimally acquire the national language—enough to feel superior to the elders of their own communities; and only enough to join the ghetto masses—too ignorant of the national tongue for climbing over the higher and higher walls being erected by the preparatories and universities.

Schools and universities, monocultural or multicultural, do not eliminate ignorance, but make it functional, while suppressing difference and cultural diversity. They cannot but promote the "superstitious efficacy" of Indian cultures. This consequence is inevitable even when indigenous knowledge becomes the academic aim, while the classroom becomes the site for its transmission through education—postmodern, multicultural, or other.

Reform, Revamping, Radicalization

A common faith connects the radical Left and the conservative Right. It undergirds and overcomes the divide of deep differences that they focus upon in their battles with each other within the academy.

One key element of this common faith, professed assiduously by educators as well as all other professionals, is their capacity for solving problems. Problems are part of the human condition[3] and every self-respecting professional solves some of them. Progress brings new problems and the professions progress by solving the problems that progress deposits at the door of humanity. No self-respecting professional abandons the faith of the faithful: the profession improves the human condition, preventing stagnation or deterioration. The first profession's Hippocratic oath becomes both the touchstone and the promise of its modern descendants—all of them problem solvers. But even before the era of litigation proliferated by the legal profession, professionals have remained leery of promising their clients a rose garden—especially not one that would render redundant the professions.

The common faith shared by professional educators contains many other elements, including a certain *certainty:* education is essential for the survival and flourishing of every culture, past, present, and future. There is no exception or qualification to this universal rule. *There would and could be no cultural continuity or advancement without education.*

Whatever their political or philosophical orientation, another element which brings all educators under the roof of the same professional faith is the certainty that more education is always better than less. The more the better is the inexorable law of the professions.

More of what kind of education? This question, without threatening the common faith, cracks open the impossibility of consensus, either about the aims of education or the means that deserve to be called "educative" (Dewey 1963).

What social, personal, and other diseases must be cured by education? What types of well-being are sought? And how? Battles between the camps proliferate, with escalating violence and its victims. Professionals remain unperturbed; assuring themselves and their clients that competition among them is as natural, normal, and healthy as it is in the classroom; or, for that matter, in the world for which the classroom must be the best training ground—sorting out the strong from the weak; the lions of the jungle from the sacrificial lambs.

The Crassly Competitive

Vigor and vitality require competition, profess the promoters of bell curves, standardized tests, and other marvelous measures that separate the supermen from the mental midgets. They urge pragmatism and practicality; the stuff of the "real world": the modern or the postmodern jungle, concrete or virtual, where "the survival of the fittest"—the ancient, even primordial law—still separates the grain from the chaff; the real men from the boys; the strong and able from the weak and disabled; the winners from the losers; the first from the last; the successes from the failures who deserve their fate of working for McDonald's for minimum wage.

The As deserve the American dream. The Ds and Fs demonstrate their incapability of dreaming it. Someone has to wash the dishes in every society; fill gasoline; collect garbage; line landfills; clean out toxic dumps; spray chemicals; fill up cancer wards . . . Dropouts and Ds have earned for such jobs themselves. And the As do deserve to design worlds in which the rejects, the second rate, the bottom of the barrel do time at a job rather than filling the jails paid for by the As, the Bs and the Cs. The latter work for an honest living, rather than living off the dole; or receiving free food, health care, and the other benefits that come from serving time in jail.

In the era of globalization, those who cannot compete and win deserve to be left behind; at the receiving end of nuclear waste; of other winners' waste; slaving on plantations for winners' fruits that leave workers dead or infertile; *maquiladoras* where workers' children are born with brains hanging out of malformed skulls.

That is the real world. Get a real job with education. Or expect to be shipped out—like the other waste made by the successfully educated.

Slayers of Savage Inequalities

Tracing the trajectory of the lives lost in factories, factory farms, and jails—being built faster today than classrooms—professional slayers of savage inequalities bring us to the beginning: elementary schools with neither heat nor drip-free, dry classrooms; neither computers nor toilet paper . . . But wait. Yes, they do have the money to invest in metal detectors needed to find the knives, guns, and other weapons that "dangerous" ten- or eleven-year-olds bring to beat out each others' brains.

While the victors eat cake . . . swim in heated pools through the cold months of winter . . . lap up laptops with CD-ROMS . . . play Bach; all this complemented with individualized tending all the way to the very top of the World Trade Center where the best educators gently—oh, so gently—deliver them that they may finally start living "the dream"; charging up the future of the world with wallets full of magic plastic: it opens any shut door when the right number and expiration date are punched.

True, the law of the jungle creates victors. But, they remind us, it also creates unfortunate victims. Those victimized by inhumanely competitive races lose their humanity. So, too, do their victimizers. The dehumanization of schooling is contrary to all the highest ideals in the Western tradition of a liberal education.

A genuinely liberal education dispenses with cutthroat, crass competition; or softens the competitive edge so no one bleeds. It teaches respect for the laws of *social justice*; replaces the law of the jungle with the laws of democratic governance: creates win-win situations in which every man, woman, and child enjoys their human rights—including the right to educational *equality* and *excellence*.

Cultural Literacy Promoters

Equal opportunity or access to what? The "minimal competencies" needed for the marketplace? Or to the fragrant flowers of culture . . . the Great Books of the Western canon . . . with which one can climb to the Everests of a liberal education . . . the highest heights of "high culture"?

The reigning Czars of "high culture" remind the rest that what makes the West supreme is not merely its economic and technological superiority or prowess in the Global Economy. Equally worthy of global emulation is its great humanistic tradition, traced back to the *paideia* of Socrates and the other Ancient Greeks.

The Ancient Greeks were fine . . . but for the fact that they were pagans and had too many imperfect gods . . . lotus-eaters, womanizers, and the like. Secular cultural literacy leaves the Religious Right uneasy. Believers of the One Best Religion and the One True God agree that cultural literacy is important for promoting the One Best System of education. It must, however, be underscored that the "high culture" taught by this system does not start with the *Iliad* and the *Odyssey*. It begins with the *Bible*.

Multicultural Literacies

Raging from within the bastion of professional education, multicultural educators focus on the classroom site for suppressing the savage inequalities that leave some individuals more equal than others; and, some cultures more excellent than others.

The classroom offers the diminutive handheld mirror for studying the sickness of the larger society; the global malady. It is the immediate site for transformation; for healing social ills: the age-old saga of human oppression . . . five hundred years of colonialism as well as all the earlier modes of oppression (particularly of women and slaves) that precede as well as follow it as contemporary neocolonialism. Their long sad history of human oppression tells how White Man's pedagogy maintains his supremacy. But White Man has not been the only villain in the Play of Human Evil. Feminists, Gays and Lesbians, and the People of Color reveal Brown, Yellow, or Pink villains and victims; each group voicing their own narratives of victimization—spanning class, caste, color, age, or sexual orientation/preference.

Radicalized and reunited under the universal banner of "the pedagogy of the oppressed," they denounce all the reform efforts that give new life to "the pedagogies of the Oppressor." Instead, they call for liberation from all the diverse modes of oppression; for pedagogies and curricula that will break the long, tragic, painful history of the "Cultures of Silence." Radical democracy, social justice and liberation, recognizing lines of gender, race, color, and sexual orientation, require radical education. Authentic multicultural education conscientizes learners to the language used to justify oppressing the oppressed, rendering transparent the categories of the oppressor: "failures," "Ds and Duds," "uncivilized," "pagans," "underachievers," "underdeveloped" . . .

Multicultural educators take on today's burdens of racism, sexism, ageism, classism . . . struggling to see a million flowers bloom. Emerging from under the weight of the White Man's burden, the Rainbow Coalition points the way towards radical democracy; fully conscious that the United Colors of the Rainbow may not be possible. For there is always the brute reality of racism and monoculturalism, summing up multiculturalism as: "the label for all those groups who have failed to make it in America" (Gordon and Newfield 1994, 33).

The supremacists' arrogance and intolerance must not be succumbed to. Multicultural education must continue to wage the battle for difference and diversity in the classroom. Furthermore, education is a basic need, necessity, and right.

* * *

These four reformation camps are but rough, broad categories for contemporary professional fix-its. They reveal the mere tip of the proverbial iceberg. There are at least as many cures as there are identified educational ills. As with the medical establishment, there is prestige for every new disease discovered and treated: community destruction can be cured by communitarian education; low self-esteem can be raised by empowering education; racism can be cured by antiracist pedagogies; fragmentation can be fixed by interdisciplinary or holistic education; regimentation can be reversed by pedagogies for play; environmental damage can be healed by environmental education. . . .

The required or recommended course readings for these fixes not only nourish the publication industry; they fatten the curriculum vitae of every new educational reformer who first identifies the mysterious ill that prohibits the desired learning; and then finds a pedagogical and curricular cure for it. Among the vast and growing educational reformers, the most *respectable* are certainly the great masters of alchemy who promise better schools. The most *seductive* are the popular magicians who promise to make every kitchen into an alchemical laboratory. The most *sinister* are the new masons of the universe who want to transform the entire world into one huge temple of learning (Illich 1977, 72–73 emphasis added).

* * *

To reform or to abandon education?

That is *the* question that no respectable professional dares to ask without facing the threat of disrepute.

Committed professionals cannot confess, even in the privacy of their bedrooms, let alone in the public arena, that all the cures concocted by their profession are far, far more terrible than all the different diseases they profess to heal.

Heretics who dare to deprofessionalize themselves must be put to death; or, best yet, either not be studied at all or be studied just enough to merit dismissal with a sound kick in the pants so that students learn proper obedience and respect for the professions.

It is a valuable lesson for learners to see that in the Open Society, serious critics of the professions are given enough room to jest, like the professional jesters of the court, in order to be soundly jeered out of the critical professional consciousness.

Multicultural Education: An Oxymoron

American pluralism has a beautiful but limited tradition. Its enormous variety of educational, medical and ecclesial systems witness to it. . . . Only in the domain of religion is the constitutional protection of the non-churched atheist taken seriously. This society is gravely threatened unless we recognize, without envy sublimated into grudge, that dropouts of any description might be closer to Huck Finn than are the churchgoers or schoolgoers (Illich 1996, 258).

Corruptio Optima Quae Est Pessima. The corruption of the best is the worst.

Multicultural education aspires for the richest aims yet to be conceived in the history of the educational system. Who but the Hitlers, the Pol Pots, the Pinochets, the white supremacists, the Ku Klux Klan, the *Ananda Margis,* the Shining Path, and other fundamentalists can resist or deny its allure and enchantment; of aims that seek to humanize through multiculturalizing a system in which more than half the children become human waste; dropouts or human droppings?

That question provokes us to ask whether multicultural education is an example of Promethean expectations gone awry? Is it possible that an expensive system—unaffordable for the Two-Thirds World—which has failed abysmally to teach "the basics" (the three modern Rs) is being given the noble responsibility of passing on all the other rich elements of culture by multicultural educators? Is it possible that the system that cannot transmit the culture of *homo monolinguis* with minimal competence is being asked to transmit the 5,000 spoken cultures that constitute the richness of the lived pluriverse at the grassroots—of the noneducated and the uneducated? Is the school cafeteria that cannot present hot dogs and hamburgers palatably to be the chosen political site for cultural workers serving *bhojan, comida,* or the other elaborate edible cultural delicacies fully and inextricably embedded in the commons of the pluriverse?[4]

Undoubtedly, many multicultural educators reflect the best sentiments and ideals found today within the educational system of *homo monolinguis:* aspiring to instruct about other landscapes of learning without deprecation; without reducing others' rites of passage as either touristic exotica or Stage One in the historical evolution of the educational system. Still, the multicultural classroom, however celebratory or respectful of cultural diversity, can only be a deliberately western site; transmitting *only* the culture/s of the West. In that limited capacity, while very useful for western "cultural workers" taking their first steps in hosting and hospitality toward the Otherness of the Other, it cannot do anything in terms of initiation into the cultures of the pluriverse. The pluriverse of cultural diversity cannot be nourished or regenerated through the project of education. For education is of modern western origin. Multicultural education is an oxymoron.

Learning and teaching preceded education and the educational system by millennia. The *paideia* of the Greeks or the *gyan* and *gurushishya parampara* of the Hindus of Hindustan must not be equated with education. The reduction of the former to the education of modern man and woman, or its importation into any brand of multicultural education is tantamount to colonization.

[T]he word 'education' is of recent coinage. It was unknown before the Reformation. The education of children is first mentioned in French in a document of 1498. This was the year when Erasmus settled in Oxford, when Savonarola was burned at the stake in Florence, and when Dürer etched his *Apocalypse,* which speaks to us powerfully about the sense of doom hanging over the end of the Middle Ages. In the English language the word 'education' first appeared in 1530—the year when Henry VIII divorced Catherine of Aragon and when the Lutheran Church separated from Rome at the Diet of Augsburg. In Spanish lands another century passed before the word and idea of education became known. In 1632 Lope de Vega still refers to 'education' as a novelty. That year, the University of San Marcos in Lima celebrated its sixtieth anniversary. Learning centers did exist before the term 'education' entered common parlance. You 'read' the classics or the law; you were not educated for life (Illich 1977, 75).

"In Lieu of Education" (Illich 1977) documents how the western (and, therefore, modern) mind coopts and colonizes the Other—whether of the historical past or the contemporary present—in and through reducing their pluriverse of diverse and incommensurable cultural patterns and styles of teaching and learning, placing them under the universal umbrella called "education."

While the global mission of the Church is to save souls, the global mission of the educational system is secular salvation. The noblest variety of secular salvation saves the mind of the individual from remaining stunted or from rotting; while the most "practical" or "pragmatic" is defined by the market for employment: the holy "job market." Education shares other elements with Religion.

> Schooling and education are related to each other like Church and religion, or in more general terms, like ritual and myth; it is mythopoetic, and the myth generates the curriculum through which it is perpetuated. Education, as the designation for an all embracing category of social justification, is an idea for which we cannot find (outside Christian theology) a specific analogue in other cultures. And the production of education through the process of schooling sets schools apart from other institutions for learning that existed in other epochs (Illich 1977, 76).

Illich's historical journeys into noneconomic cultures, western and other, help us discover that *homo educandus* is necessarily *homo oeconomicus*—a modern mutant in the East as in the West. *Homo educandus* represents the historical emergence of a new kind of human being: who *needs* education in order to learn or live well. *Homo educandus* radically differs from *homo sapiens* or *homo faber.*

"[T]he idea that man was born incompetent for society and remained so unless he was provided with 'education'" became a new consensus among the elites in the West only in the early seventeenth century. With the spread of this modern "certainty," education came to mean

> the inverse of vital competence. It came to mean a process rather than the plain knowledge of the facts and the ability to use tools which shape a man's concrete life. Education came to mean an intangible commodity that had to

be produced for the benefit of all, and imparted to them in the manner in which the visible Church formerly imparted invisible grace. Justification in the sight of society became the first necessity for a man born in *original stupidity,* analogous to *original sin* (Illich 1977, 75–76, emphases added).

For the uneducated or noneducated or miseducated social majorities, their own ways of life are genuine alternatives to the progressive pollution, exploitation, and opaqueness now observed in rich countries. But "the dethroning of GNP cannot be achieved without simultaneously subverting GNE—Gross National Education, usually conceived as manpower capitalization" (Illich 1977, 90–91).

To resist GNE, alternatives to education are both necessary and available in the Two-Thirds world. Realizing this in the beginning of the twentieth century, Gandhi offered *Nai Talim* (often translated as "New Education") as an antidote to the education of the brown "intimate enemy" (Nandy 1981) as well as the White pedagogue. Gandhi's *Nai Talim* keeps alive his peoples' subsistence economy. It celebrates the richness and the dignity of bread labor—which weaves more strongly the fabric of the local community, emphasizing the autonomy and self-sufficiency needed to marginalize the economy of *homo oeconomicus* and *homo educandus. Nai Talim* teaches *Yama-Niyam;* the regeneration of *Varna Vyavastha; the sanskriti* of *dharma* . . . nurturance *of buddhi* . . . *Jnana (Gyana)* . . . *atmagyana.* None of these ideals are translatable into the language of educators (Gandhi 1946, 1970; Prakash 1993; Vora 1993).

The "bread labor" central to *Nai Talim* keeps pyramidal hierarchies at bay. Economic social pyramids are incompatible with the common sense of *Nai Talim. Bhaniya pan ghaniya nahin,* observe Gandhi's fellow Gujratis, when speaking of people who possess education, while lacking sense and sensibility. In fact our study of education reveals that wherever people abandon their own forms of cultural initiation, they lose their *common sense;* their cultural sense and sensibility developed in their *commons.* Since Aristotle and until the seventeenth century, common sense was the sense bringing harmony and correspondence to all other senses. It should not be looked for in the pineal gland, as Descartes suggested; or in the universal reason proposed by Bacon. Common sense is what people have in common; the sense that can be found only in community. Gandhi's common sense tells him, as Illich's common sense reveals for us today, that an "egalitarian economy cannot exist in a society in which the right to produce is conferred by schools" (Illich 1977, 91).

Multicultural education promises all cultures a more equal share of the educational pie constituted of the nonsubsistence economy—national, international, and global—whether liberal, socialist, or neoliberal. Undoubtedly, multicultural education is a step forward in the educated person's quest for better representation; for more inclusion; for less violence; for more respect. Unfortunately, these ideals are aspired for within the very economic system that wipes out other economies—of household, commons, and community; sustaining, thereby, the educators' mythopoesis: that there are no authentic alternatives TO education; that education is a universal good; that, therefore, the educational system, currently broken, must be reformed and revamped. The same system that helped smash the languages, customs, and traditions of the commons can be reformed to teach the knowledge and skills required to build communities; or be reformulated to nourish a pluriverse.

Multicultural educators run with the fox while hunting with the hound. Empowering individuals, communities, and cultures, multicultural educators promise equal educational opportunities—personal, communal, and cultural—for joining the global project of education . . . defined by the mindset of *homo educandus*, with his moral language of Human Rights.

Human Rights: The Contemporary Trojan Horse

Human rights are only 200 years old. The ideology and the institutional arrangements of human rights were born after unprecedented forms of social and personal deprivation took root among the "developed" peoples and places of this planet. The regime of the nation-state, fusing nationalism and statehood, was constructed at this same time, to keep the social order in a society exposed to the forces of the modern market, reducing the human condition to that of *homo oeconomicus*.

The birth of universal human rights is inextricably bound up with the global manufacture of the independent western nation-state. Following five centuries of colonialism, the post-World War II universalization of this western institution continues to deal severe blows to all other political organizations; most particularly the commons cared for or "administered" through village self-governance. The evils and injustices of traditional village governance, masterfully documented by

Achebe (1961, 1985) and others, are minuscule in scale or severity when compared with those of national governments. Yet these as well as their contemporary descendants, the transborder corporate super-structures constituting the "Global Project," are being legitimized as those responsible to uphold and safeguard the Gospel of human rights.

In the era of the global economy, not even the Great Wall of China poses an obstacle to the universalization of human rights. Thousands of determined participants fly over the Wall into Beijing to attend the Fourth UN Conference on Human/Women's Rights, intent upon their universalization, spreading them to every corner of the globe.[5] Grander and more global than all the other conferences now regularly held from Malaysia to Mexico to promote human rights, its participants seek to liberate and bring justice to all the oppressed peoples of the earth. This justice calls for bringing one and all under the care of the global classroom for disseminating education.

For villages or cities across the globe, the moral currency of universalizable human rights is being newly minted, promising even to contain the immoralities of State governments (national or local) as well as international development agencies. This moral currency, con-ceived and created for the abstract "citizen," follows Hobbes in con-taining their meanness, brutality, greed, and envy; while enjoining duties, obligations, and responsibilities toward fellow citizens and flags. It replaces the traditional communal morality of peoples not reduced to modern individualism, either old or new (Dewey 1962). Function-ing like the British pound, the American dollar, and other "hard" cur-rencies, this equally "hard" moral coinage of human rights enjoys the same international status of preeminence as do the other coins of the economically "developed." Both monetary and moral currencies of the "developed" destroy and devalue the "soft" currencies of commu-nities and peoples considered not only economically but also morally underdeveloped. Following the colonial path of Christian missionaries (who saved primitive souls from pagan gods), their descendants, the delegates of human rights agencies, offer secular salvation: the moral or economic development of underdeveloped cultures. "One man one vote"–style democracy with parliaments or senates, a national economy that manufactures classrooms, courts, patients' wards, sewage, tele-phones, jobs, and flush toilets are only some of the liberty and welfare rights promised by independent modern States. At the nexus stand the classrooms of school, college, and university.

This style of "national independence" is incompatible with cultural autonomy.

[H]ow easily under the cloak of 'Human Rights' a particular 'civilization' may penetrate into others and disrupt the fabric of different cultures . . . We can strive for success in international markets, but no people can live from a borrowed myth . . . No culture, tradition, ideology, or religion can today speak for the whole of humankind, let alone solve its problems . . . Human Rights is the fruit of a very partial dialogue among the cultures of the world (Panikkar 1995, 112–113).

Human rights are social constructions or cultural *inventions*. They are not, as some adherents claim, natural discoveries.[6] Human rights are but the formal, juridical expression of a *specific* mode of being and living. They are defined by the kind of man, woman, and child who has appeared on earth only very recently: *Homo oeconomicus,* the possessive individual. First born and brought up in the West, this modern "person"—the individual self—is now threatening the whole world with the plague of endless needs, legitimized under the moral mask of human rights.[7]

We need to be aware that the very notion of right and law is a western notion . . . It is but a window among others on the world, an instrument of communication and a language among others. The word not only is non-existent among the indigenous traditional cultures, but it will never come to their minds that human beings can have rights. . . . For them, it is difficult to understand that rights or entitlements could be homocentrically defined by a human being. That they, furthermore, could be defined by a sovereign state, that is, by a collection of sovereign individuals, is almost ridiculous (Vachon 1990, 165).

The processes that created *Homo oeconomicus* (the possessor of human rights) disembedded the economy from commons, community, and culture, while constituting it as an autonomous sphere. These processes "evolved" and mutated over almost a thousand years (Polanyi 1975). After the enclosure of the commons, there occurred a radical rupture with the traditional past. Some describe this rupture as the transition to the capitalist mode of production (Marx); others as the transition from the aegis of gender to the regime of sex (Illich); and still others as the birth of the modern age. Economic man was born after this rupture. The individual self was created before, apparently with the invention of the text (Illich 1987a, 1993), but he was still immersed in a religious cosmology (Cougar 1973). The economic individual, a new genderless being, mobilized principally by self-interest, and dedicated to optimizing his behavior (the rational use of scarce means for unlimited ends), could only acquire his place in history when the idea of equality had become a popular prejudice (Marx), and when the assumption of scarcity, which the patron saints of economics transformed into a social law (Esteva 1980, 1992), had been established as a governing principle of society.

This "evolution" has transmogrified peoples and cultures so profoundly that previous virtues are now reduced to vices, and traditional vices have been elevated to virtues. Hopes have been transformed into expectations; the richness of tradition into a burden; wisdom into backwardness; awareness of self-limitation into apathy or lack of initiative; frugality into the inability to compete for the maximization of utility; envy into the motivation that heralds progress and economic growth (Dumont 1977; Esteva 1992; MacIntyre 1981; Orr 1992). Vitality, the daily expression of the condition of being alive in and through being entwined or intertwined with others and the world, has been transformed into mimetic desire (Girard 1978) to "catch up" and compete. Desires have been transformed into needs, and needs into rights.

The nation-state, as a political regime constructed to put order in the operation of the national economy, was constituted as a social pact among individuals, to whom it attributed, for the simple fact of being members of the State, the right or the *entitlement* (Sen 1981) to the satisfaction of their needs by the Market or the State. Looking for the modern definition of human nature, we discover *needy man:* dependent on economic goods and services—the objects that satisfy his needs for survival and flourishing. The tautology of the modern definition of human beings is their subordination to the laws of scarcity.

The founding fathers of economics saw in *scarcity* the keystone for their theoretical constructions. They postulated it as a universal condition of human society, with axiomatic value. Economists have even been able to transform their finding into a popular prejudice, a self-evident truism for everyone. "Common sense" is now so immersed in the notions of economic "rationality" that it is very difficult to recognize the economists' premise of "scarcity" or "rationality" as mere leftovers of modern science; words which, like others, fell into and colonized ordinary language and perception.

Wherever the law of scarcity is already enforced as the necessary accompaniment of economic principles, a social space is created for demanding the enforcement of some variety of human rights. But the demand for the universalization of these rights is also advancing through contagion into spheres where they still express the protection of freedoms. Once the scarcity of schools and teachers is established through the redefinition of learning and preparation for living, the right to compulsory schooling is enforced. The recent scarcity of human organs (for transplants) or genes (for genetic engineering) has already created the debate about the corresponding rights, which are starting to be included in national and international codes. Freedoms like those associated with cultural practices (in birth, marriage, or death, for example) are increasingly formulated in terms of rights.

The final step in the global takeover by the monoculture of human rights is now the object of an international debate. Loud voices are currently claiming that the "community of nations," the United Nations, should be endowed with powers and resources to apply the global right of intervention anywhere on earth "for humanitarian purposes": that is, with the explicit object of protecting human rights. The codification of that new right formally breaks one of this century's international rules, based on the principles of peoples' self-determination and protection from foreign intervention in national affairs. Highly controversial, this "right" is being recognized as one more way to legitimize colonial interventions.

This charge, by now well founded and documented, expresses the very essence of human rights as colonial tools for domination. Colonialism always implied a kind of moral and political violation, something imposed by the brute force of the physically strong, with different kinds of ideological emblems used to legitimize such violation. The Cross coming with the Sword took different shapes—like development or democracy in the postwar era. What is now under discussion would amount to the final consecration of the legal and legitimate right of colonial intervention . . . in the name of human rights.

We are aware that in packing into a few paragraphs such a complex transformation of the human condition, we leave ourselves vulnerable to the charge of controversial oversimplifications and interpretations. We assume that risk in order to give the bare outlines of a sketch without which few can appreciate our concern and our hope for the end of the global encroachment sought by the regime of these rights in general, and the welfare and liberty right to education, in particular.

The Nexus of Contemporary Domination: Education–Human Rights–Development

Education and human rights belong to the same discourse as development, with its web of familiar key terms and concepts: human resources, the global economy, growth, technology, progress, planning, production, science, standard of living, One World, participation, empowerment and democracy (Sachs 1992). Some of these key terms, like development or human resources have been around for only a few scant decades. Others, like education, are almost five hundred years old. Still others go back further yet—but now have transmogrified modern and postmodern meanings. Because of these recent meanings, all the terms and concepts of the education-development dictionary bear a certain family resemblance, belonging to the same vast family of modern or postmodern ideas and ideals. They reign supreme within the centers of the academy, as well as in the economy served by it.

Rather than calling it a family, it is more accurate to say that this conglomerate of ideas and ideals belongs to a growing net: grand, vast, and global. The master weavers—educators, development planners, programmers, and other professionals—sit in classrooms, offices, and factories, weaving this great global net of education and development; of modern and postmodern cosmovisions floated into cyberspace; yet presented as down to earth and profoundly practical.

Keeping clear of God-given Edens, this mythopoesis reveals peoples of all places and cultures pulling themselves up by their educated bootstraps, joining the human quest for progress. This global net promises the whole world a full forthcoming catch: cleansing the land and the oceans of poverty and overpopulation, parochialism and bigotry, violence and oppression. With these ills strained out of the *conditio humana,* the "human family" can begin to enjoy the gains of empowerment and emancipation in the "global village"—decidedly democratic, multicolored, and multicultural.

In the reality separated from such myths by a grand chasm, wherever education and development travel (hand in hand), poverty and pollution increase; freedoms and autonomy decrease; monocultures of learning and living destroy the rich pluriverse of the diverse cultures of the social majorities. In the reality beyond such mythos, this vast industrial net does not catch and trap ills. Instead, it catches cultures; dragging out of their embedded cultural contexts the wondrous variety found in the lived pluriverse of teaching and learning, work and leisure, ritual and ceremony, food and dance, healing and dying, as well as all other cultural practices. Wrenched and uprooted from their traditional spaces, indigenous knowledge, skills and the arts of dwellers are trapped, killed, and frozen; to be microwaved and eaten in the fifty-minute period that lies between the bell that initiates class and the bell that terminates it.

As the dawning millennium manufactures new educational technologies, the scale and speed of the cultural catch gets bigger and quicker; similar to the catches currently threatening global industrial fisheries. The Destroyer is being destroyed by his own dance. This industry, joined by other forces of development and progress, is contaminating all the waters of the world with such success that even the creatures outside the net are threatened, endangered, or totally destroyed.

A growing minority of educators are recognizing the contamination and damage of the net cast by global development and education. Some seek to "green" education with interdisciplinary programs for ecological literacy. Others proffer multicultural literacies as a way for dispensing with the net of cultural and ecological destruction. Just as peace educators, fighting for disarmament, propose that education teach people to transform weapons of war into plough shares, multicultural educators propose tearing up the educational net that traps, kills, and destroys the cultures of the marginals, the dropouts, the silent ones. They teach themselves and their students to "think globally" rather than parochially; to become global citizens; to broaden their consciousness, extending their sympathies beyond the confines of national and cultural boundaries, embracing the Other in the global village.

We take heart from the efforts of all those working within the educational system to open up its doors, shut for centuries to the challenge of respecting the Other, to the survival and flourishing of cultural diversity. However, the further we walk beyond these doors being opened by critical multicultural educators, the deeper we enter landscapes of learning not marred by industrial civilization, the better we understand why authentic cultural practices are necessarily taught outside the classroom; there where the notion of the profession has no meaning. The more respectfully we explore these cultural practices, the more clearly we discover the reasons why it is impossible to package the cultures of the other for transmission and consumption in the global classroom. Packaged for transportation to and consumption within the classroom, they must be severely uprooted; severed from the soils and waters, the ecological or natural niches where they are born and the commons and community without which they must die out. Rendered extinct.

Multiculturalizing the classroom cannot save soil cultures from such a fate. However passionately committed to cultural diversity, the classroom must necessarily be the cemetery of sensibilities cultivated in commons and communities, central to the transmission and regeneration of soil cultures. Deities in stone and wood, stolen or bought "dirt cheap" from the peoples who worship them and sold to the museums of the West, become "priceless art." In the course of making this journey from the familiar world of shrines and temples into the alien world of museums, they are reduced from being worshipped goddesses of immeasurable power into the art, artifacts, and objects of another culture that emphasizes economic and aesthetic value, rather than spiritual significance. True, the deities of savages are safer in the museums that house and guard them with alarm systems and uniformed guards, keeping them out of the hands of thieves and marauders who sold them to the museums in the first place. But while preserving them from the processes of natural destruction and debilitation, they are radically transmogrified. Instead of being daily nurtured and worshipped with food and prayer, these deities sit behind glass; objects of serious research and study, or even plain and vulgar gawking by self-styled aficionados or "culture vultures."[8] The multicultural class threatens the cultures of the Other with a similar fate; seeking as they do to become the global site for cultural initiation.

The project of global development, only five decades old, offers an excellent perspective for deconstructing all contemporary multicultural efforts in educational reform.[9] In the global race for a spot in the Global Economy, Mauritania will take 3,223 years to "catch up" with the U.S.—we have heard development experts pronounce. By dropping out of the global race for development, by being themselves, Mauritanians are recovering their dignity TODAY. They do not have to wait for 3,223 years!

To be themselves, most of the peoples on earth (the social majorities) do not need education. Like all other modern "needs," the need for education has been a creation of the "disabling professions," privileged by their enterprise. People do not *need* to breathe when they are breathing; only when they are drowning, or otherwise deprived of breathable air. Similarly, in order to acquire modern "needs," people must first be deprived of their conditions for the good life of subsistence—in all of its diverse definitions. De-skilled (Braverman 1975) or weaned from their subsistence economy, they fall into the trap of needing a job, savings, welfare, daycare. . . . Once their dignity or competence is no longer accepted or recognized without a diploma, they begin to need education. The destruction of the conditions of a subsistent good life is required to create education and the other "needs" of a very specific, culturally determined, life style—now established as a universal goal, transforming every man and woman into a needy subject with rights or claims for the satisfaction of those "needs."

To be themselves, free of the needs of needy *homo educandus,* the social majorities rely upon their own traditions of cultural initiation. Contrary to the myths of (professional) educators, the traditions of the Other are neither stagnant nor parochial. They have their predicaments, their limitations, their demonic dimensions. Yet, they also contain within themselves the seeds for their own reform and regeneration; revealing the fact that "genius" is not the scarce commodity that only a few possess, but is abundantly and generously spread across cultures. This is neither to romanticize nor to turn a blind eye to the savage side of each cultural group. It is to recognize that just as savagery and violence are pretty widely distributed across all cultures, so is the genius to solve the predicaments experienced and faced differently in the pluriverse.

Apologies and Celebration

Prestigious places for locking things up, museums [and classrooms] are outside of life: in this way they resemble cemeteries (Hainard and Kaer 1986, 33).

Among the people we deeply respect and cherish, some call themselves multicultural educators, while others call themselves human rights activists. Are we betraying our colleagues, friends, and others for whom we feel enormous affection and admiration? Are we betraying ourselves and our work within the educational system?

Among our memorable teachers of our childhood as well as our adult years, we remember several priests with profound love and respect. They were sent as missionaries to convert the pagans of the Third World. With hindsight, we recognize that they did the opposite of what their bosses intended for them. Their respect for our ways offered a welcome respite from the evangelisms of their colleagues. Refusing to push their God on us, they celebrated our pagan gods with us. Without embracing our pagan gods as theirs, they joined us in nourishing our pluriverse. In their eyes, we saw we needed no salvation. Their hospitality to our religion extended itself to the other dimensions of our cultures. While they taught in school, they did not teach school. They did not try to school or educate us. They did not try to conscientize or empower us.[10]

Instead, in their gaze, we saw our own power reflected; no one had to give us the power we already possessed. We exercised it by tapping into our own capacities for courage, faith, and hope. In the spaces we created together, sheltered from institutional authority, we could be ourselves—unique, personally, or culturally. Seeing ourselves reflected in their eyes, we learned to celebrate the singularity and particularity of our commons, commonness, common sense.

In and through these I–Thou encounters, we learned what it means to be hospitable to the Otherness of the Other. Because they embraced our Shiv, Ganesh, or Ganapati, our Votan, we took their Christ as one of our *huacas*. Our pluriverse was enriched by the encounter with theirs; as theirs was enriched by the encounter with ours. Neither educated the other. These encounters with the culture of the Other, through intercultural dialogues,[11] took us deeper into our own cultures—beyond education.

It is said that "the truest eye may now belong to the migrant's double vision" (Bhabha 1997, 30). If there is even a tiny grain of truth in that observation, then the pain of migrations between the different worlds we traverse may yet bear some fruit. . . . Even the bittersweet ones may be savored and enjoyed.

Following in the footsteps of these open, cherished teachers, we seek not to impose our rejection on anyone. We know very well that education for jobs, like the family car and flush toilet, is felt as a basic needs for many millions. They cannot survive, or have the good life as they understand it, if that need is not satisfied by the Market or the State. They cannot conceive their own way of living without the consumption of goods and services now defining their survival kits. We are not arguing that they be deprived of their "rights" to satisfy their "needs." All we are emphasizing is our solidarity with the millions saying "No, thanks" to all those "needs" and "rights"—thus rejecting the universality of development and education. Inspired by the diversity of the lived pluriverse, we seek *limits* for education and *respect* for different ways of living, learning, and teaching, through political controls. These reveal to us the importance of abandoning oxymorons like multicultural education. We locate our hopes for preventing cultural meltdown in the lived pluriverse.

All those who want to bring the whole world under the umbrella of human rights insist that that is the only way to satisfy the basic needs which define people *qua* human beings. Education fulfills one of these needs. In the wake of education, the cultures of subsistence collapse. Education is not the only human right that does them in. All the human rights claimed and awarded to the modern individual self have the same devastating impact on those whose cultures of subsistence have allowed them to marginalize the economy. Human rights are as much of an historical fact as are education and *homo educandus*. In the story of humans on earth, the notion of education as a human right has a clearly identified beginning. Therefore, it can have an end.

The end is being written into the epic of the people at the grassroots.

The social majorities have next to no school. They will have neither school nor family car, flush toilet, and other pieces of the American dream—if the Club of Rome and other reports are telling the truth. Structural impossibilities prevent its universalization. That is their blessing. They do not have to be deschooled; for they have never been schooled. The goodness, the adequacy, the richness of all the reasons given for deschooling are daily demonstrated to us by the social majorities, creating their footpaths beyond the superhighways of education by walking them. They daily demonstrate for us that their languages, their traditions, their cultures subsist without the huge bureaucracies that trap the educated, faithfully running the educational race to be Number One.

Hosting the Otherness of the Other

No expert knows everything about every place, not even everything about any place (Berry 1990, 5).

The only true and effective 'operator's manual for spaceship earth' is not a book that any human will ever write; it is hundreds of thousands of local cultures (Berry 1990, 166).

It takes a whole village to raise a Zapoteco or a Punjabi child. We have heard that the same view is held by other peoples. Within the setting of the classroom, how do we bring you into our cultural space, revealing what it means to be a Punjabi or a Zapoteco?

Every time we enter the classroom, it is akin to being in cyberspace. We know we have stepped outside the realms of our cultural spaces.

How do we initiate you into our cultures in classrooms, whether in or out of cyberspace?

It takes a whole village. . . . No, we cannot go it alone—classroom style—to teach you about ourselves. Within the classroom, we cannot be of much use to you in your quest to enter our cultural space. Then how can we presume to initiate you in your culture—let alone the culture of the unknown Other?

We know that we do not know how to bring you along to savor the flavors of our vernacular worlds. We know that the lived pluriverse—of spoken vernacular tongues, of feasts and flavors, of suffering and celebrating—cannot be reduced to *information*. It is too rich, alive, and vibrant to be keyed into the memory bits and bytes that run the educational industry today.

This reveals to us our inability to be genuine guides in the rich worlds of others' cultures. To enter those worlds, only the communities themselves and their elders can be good guides: those who know how to raise the young to maturity without classrooms and textbook experts; how to sing the river *sutras;* how to remember the tongues with which they speak with the deer, the otter, and the bear; how to grow the corn so that the soils never depart; how to harvest a whole year's food with three inches of rainfall; how to make a gift of soil while we only know how to make human waste; who feel no need for lawns, yoghurt makers, or even air conditioners when temperatures soar to 140 degrees in the shade; who know how to speak to the trees and plants; who have a hundred different words for snow; who can grow four hundred species of potatoes in one small village; who know . . . all the things that we cannot imagine . . . not even in our dreams. . . . To Thou and thine we express our shared hopes of finding the strength and courage to walk away from the mirages of global prosperity created by education.

If you do not want to be reduced into the individual self stitching together his own individual designer-made or sewed-up cultural identity (Bhabha 1994), you are not alone; you are a part of quests being embarked upon by millions.

The social majorities are not fools even if they are not "learned." Without being learned, they are learning to be wary of the mirage of equal educational opportunity that earlier on seduced them from their places. They are learning to stay home, regenerating the ways of their cultures, by walking on the footpaths of their dead, their elders. They have not forgotten their cultures, their landscapes of teaching and learning that lie outside the classroom. They know that the latter cannot be encased within the limits and confines of books, libraries, museums, computers, and the other tools of their oppressors. Standing on their own soils, they need no experts to teach them how to nurture and be nurtured by their worlds.

We humbly acknowledge our ignorance before you. We cannot bear to keep you in our expert educators' clutches. Go forth with our good will to what you already have . . . with eyes wide open to the cultural traps created by the human rights-education-development-progress global net.

We hope you and your descendants will enjoy the dignity of your tribe, your culture, your places, your ways of living and learning to regenerate your spaces. We hope we will not seek to smother your cultural spaces with our certainties; nor you, ours.

We hope you will be hospitable to our ways. And we, to yours.

Notes

1   For an account of alternatives to modern law and punishment among the North American Indians, see Lauderdale 1991.

2   For a detailed analytic study of the counterproductivity of the educational system, see Green 1980.

3   The word "problem" was used in geometry to define a puzzle of logic with only one solution. It is now a plastic word (Pörksen 1995), without specific denotation. Among its connotations, it alludes to real life predicaments, difficulties, situations, that a professional can formulate as a "problem" whose "solution" necessarily includes professional advice.

4   For an extended discussion of the cultures of community embedded comida, see Esteva and Prakash, 1997.

5   See the "Platform for Action" that emerged out of the UN Fourth World Conference. Each statement of the 12-Point Platform is either an expression of concern regarding the violence against women, or a demand for universalizing the rights enjoyed by the economically privileged in the "developed" world.

6   "Natural rights" were claimed as the foundation for the creation of the modern nation-state. They are no longer legitimate. In this century, it is accepted that universal human rights are the product of reason and agreement, a covenant. How, then, can they be universal if the majority of people on earth do not share that culturally specific reason and did not take part in the covenant? The United Nations Charter is claimed to be signed by "We, the Peoples . . . " It was convened only by governments, which can speak in the name of their peoples only in formal, legal terms. For the current discussion on human rights, see International Conference on Rethinking Human Rights 1994.

7   On the history of individualism and Homo oeconomicus, see Louis Dumont 1977. For a penetrating critique of the monoculturalism inherent in the notion of human rights, and a defense of radical pluralism, see Raimundo Panikkar, especially 1995, and Vachon 1990, 1991, and 1995b.

8   The American Indians and the "community of the Museums" clashed when the latter was trying to establish its code of ethics for their collections on Indian culture. They argued, using the language of rights.

 For the museums, a) a people has the right to learn about the history of mankind, not only about its own ethnic group; b) the Indians do not give much importance to the body, but to the spirit; and c) the museums work in the name of science.

 For the Indians, a) collecting "cultural elements" represents profanation and racism; b) life is a cycle, starting with birth and ending with death, a cycle that cannot be broken; and c) culture is more important than science.

Discussing the return of Indian artifacts to their original places, the museums argued against that idea: a) if that were to happen, in a century no one will be able to learn about religious objects (which the museums have the responsibility to protect); b) these objects are not pertinent only to their producers; c) the Indians do not know how to conserve these objects—calling all of them "sacred"; d) all the objects taken by the community of museums are studied in a respectful way.

The Indians counterargued: a) the sacred objects have a key importance for the survival of Indian cultures, and they are a lot more important to perpetuate them than for the education of new generations of Whites; b) they were the *original* producers of the objects; c) the museums cannot be against the sacred values, according to which the objects "devour themselves"; d) they should only be studied and interpreted by the tribal peoples whose objects they are. The Indians also pointed out that their cultures do not have a word for "religion:" "spiritual thinking, values, and duties are entirely integrated to social, cultural, and artistic aspects in daily life. That unity of thinking is the Indian 'religion'."

The whole discussion was documented and examined in Cardoso 1990.

9   While not describing his project of ecological literacy as "multicultural," David Orr offers an interesting explanation for why education and ecological regeneration are incompatible; why "environmental education is an *oxymoron*" (Orr 1992, 149).

10   Some human rights activists are joining in solidarity with others to struggle against human rights violations without educating them in their catechism. The national or international laws are but a power abuse, imposed on all people, who ignore them or actively oppose them. Violations of human rights amount to an abuse of the abuse. It seems legitimate to struggle against them, if and when such struggle does not convey cultural destruction. For an extended analysis of the limits of this struggle as well as an elaboration of the ways in which human rights are a contemporary Trojan horse, see Esteva and Prakash, 1997.

11   For a rigorous examination of the present conditions important or necessary for an intercultural dialogue, see Panikkar 1978, 1990, 1993, and 1995, as well as Vachon 1990, 1991/1992, and 1995a.

Part II

Grassroots Postmodernism: Refusenik Cultures

The First Intercultural Dialogue?

Para dialogar
escuchar primero.
Despues
escuchar.

For a dialogue
let's listen first.
And then,
listen.

Antonio Machado

In the year of Our Lord 1524, twelve priests belonging to the order of Saint Francis arrived in New Spain (which later became Mexico). They were sent by Pope Adrian VI and by Emperor Charles V to convert the Indians.

The priests were convinced that the conversion should only be attempted through dialogue, conversation, a peaceful confrontation, inviting and attracting "like the rain and the snow falling from heaven, without violence, not suddenly, but with gentleness and softness."

As soon as they arrived, the renowned priests started conversations with the Indian principals. A written record of those conversations was kept. Forty years later, Friar Bernardino de Sahagún, who had been trying for a long time to understand Indian thinking and culture, found those notes. He decided to give some order to the old papers and to put the text "in polished Mexican language," with the help of the best "Mexican scholars." There is not much left of what Friar Bernardino did, but there is enough to imagine what the encounter may have been.

It is the first written testimony of an attempt at dialogue among Europeans and Indians; one of the first in the world between peoples

of vastly different languages and cultures. With infinite courtesy, prominent persons on opposed sides talked. Both parties knew of the other's
regime of domination. The rank of the Franciscans clearly established
itself when Cortés, the Conqueror, the supreme authority of the Spaniards, fell on his knees in front of them. The Indians showed their lucid
acknowledgment of the objective limits of the dialogue—even as the
Franciscans repeated their tranquilizing phrases, designed to delink
the dialogue from its political context.

We have only a few pages, magnificent and fascinating, of what
was said by the Indians. They come from only one of the many "conversations." We have no more.

Learned, carefully conceived for the Indian principals (noblemen as
well as high priests), the revelations of the Franciscans clarify that
they do not seek conversion out of their own initiative or for any
mundane purpose. They are sent by God himself, through his Vicar,
and with no other motive but the salvation of the Indians' souls. Gently, ever so gently, they expose that the doctrine they bring is the
Divine Word, deposited and kept in the sacred book they have with
them. In wonderful colors, they describe all the virtues and powers of
God, as well as the miseries of the devils. To the latter, they attribute
the perverse illusion: the Indian gods, nothing more and nothing less
than despised devils, punished by God. For adoring the devil as their
gods, the Indians cannot be held guilty, not having had previous access to the Divine Word. Now, finally, they have the opportunity to
listen to the Word of God. The time has come for them to abandon
their false beliefs—for their own good, for the salvation of their souls.

The answer of the Indian principals is brief; or at least what has
been kept of it. With the fullest courtesy, the Indians acknowledge that
the priests are divine messengers; possibly even God incarnated; or
the voice and the word of Him who gives life. And God asks them to
negate their own gods, their ancient rules of life. What can they say?
How do they react to such an atrocious demand?

They have assumed themselves to be learned in the divine myster-
ies; the ones charged with interpreting them for "the queue and the
wing," for the people. At the same time, they recognize themselves as
only human, little things, limited beings, belonging to the earth:

> macehualuchos (the poorest of the poor), earthy, muddy, frayed, miserable,
> sick, afflicted. The Lord, Our Lord, only lent us a corner of his mat, of his
> site, where he placed us . . . (Sahagún 1524, 149).

They know the risk they are taking. They know they can perish, they are mortals. They have no option but to die, because their gods are dead. But even so, they will open a little the box of secrets of their gods.

In their finiteness, yet with infinite courtesy, offering the choicest phrases of their language, they reply with all firmness that they cannot accept everything being told by the Christians as Truth—even if it is the word of incarnated divinity!

The gods gave command, dominion, prestige. To them is owed life, birth, growth. A rule of life has been established and transmitted from one generation to the next.

> Are we going to destroy the ancient rule of life? (153)

There is a call for good sense, for prudence, for wisdom:

> Our lords, don't do something to your queue, your wing (your people) that bring them disgrace, that will make them perish . . . (153).

A warning:

> . . . that with this, before us, the queue and the wing (the people) may rebel . . . We may . . . act foolishly, if we so tell them: 'There is no longer a need to invoke, there is no longer a need to implore the gods' (153).

And a conclusion:

> In peace and tranquility, consider, our lords, what is needed. We cannot be calm and certainly we don't follow you. We hold that as truth, even if we offend you . . .

> It is enough that we have left, that we have lost, that we have been deprived, that we have been deposed off the mat, the seat of honor (the command) . . .

> Make with us whatever you want. That is all we answer (155).

If the command and the power have been lost, let us preserve at least the ancient rule of life, the road needed to reach nearer the gods! The priests answered:

> Don't be afraid . . . You should not take our word, what we have said, for a bad omen, how, in which way, none of your gods is a true god (155).

Immediately afterwards, the priests explained the Christian doctrine to the Indians, copiously and full of love (Sahagún 1524).

Educating the Indians

Indian peoples have been an obsession for the elites governing Mexico since its invention. Had it not been for the burden the Indian peoples represented, it was assumed, Mexico might have been as great as France or the United States.

In 1820, one of Mexico's most brilliant intellectuals, Dr. José Ma. Luis Mora, dedicated to forging the new State, asked for legislation establishing a ban on the very use of the word "Indian"—to legally suppress both the discrimination against the Indians and the very cultural condition of being an Indian. Some voices even claimed that the Mexicans should follow the example of the U.S.—not only its general political and social design, but also its handling of the Indian problem: to exterminate the majority while isolating those remaining in reservations. But there were too many Indians in Mexico—a lot more than the "Mexicans." And the elites, mainly enlightened liberals, could not even conceive of genocide U.S.-style. They imagined something better: educating the Indians—a radical, brutal culturicide.

The colonial period in Mexico ended at a time in which the creation of the nation-state, after the French and American revolutions, implied a "need" for education. The Cadiz Constitution of 1812 established the requisite of literacy to be a citizen of Spain. Many provinces in Mexico adopted the same requisite, but obstacles to the literacy campaigns soon forced their governments to grant citizenship to illiterate adults. During the first years of independent Mexico, literacy and education were assumed as fundamental conditions for the construction of the new country. For many years, however, the weakness of the unstable governments, often trapped in civil war, did not do much to fulfill their educational ideals. Their efforts were concentrated on some Lancasterian schools and centers for training workers. The great historian Lucas Alamán expressed his perplexity with the social contradictions he was observing:

> Some families send their sons to Jesuit schools in England and the United States, which presents the rare situation that the Mexican youth, in order to be brought up in entirely religious principles, go to learn to be Catholics in Protestant countries (Alamán 1852, 56).

With the restoration of the Republic by the middle of the century, after the French and American interventions, the government gave education the first priority. While the "Indian question" was still defined as the main challenge of the country, and education was identified as the only means of overcoming it, educational efforts were concentrated only on those sectors of society instructed to produce workers. The Indians were virtually forgotten or subsumed within those lowest categories that lack education. There were voices, like those of pedagogue Abraham Castellanos, who insisted on the need of providing them with education, both for their personal good and to benefit the nation. For him, as for all Indian defenders, their education included the three Rs and some technical training. Most importantly, education was to make them into "normal" citizens: fully-fledged, non-Indian members of the Mexican society.

The twentieth century dawned with celebrating the progress achieved. Mexican elites, educated in Europe or the U.S., imported their fashions, inventions, and capital to promote production and build the economic infrastructure (railroads, etc.). At the end of the first decade, the dictator Porfirio Diaz considered that the society had advanced sufficiently in economic terms, and was now ready for democracy. His resistance to it, however, detonated a liberal revolution in 1910, which soon became the first social revolution of the century. The peasant and Indian armies occupied the center of the struggle, not so much to get the suffrage asked for by the liberals, but against the oppression they were suffering and to reclaim their commons.

The revolution imposed a million deaths, in a nation numbering twelve million. It dissolved the old political regime, but failed to produce a substantial change in the economic and social structure, while leaving the country in ruins, fully disarticulated. It also produced a hybrid: the Constitution of 1917 had a liberal design but strong social commitments. The first governments emanating from the revolution sought to unite and integrate the country, creating the main institutions of modern Mexico. A new ministry was established to create a truly national system of education. Its "cultural missions," inspired by the work of the priests of the sixteenth century, brought a lay message to the last corner of the country. Its popular editions of the Western classics, published for the millions, are still remembered in the country as a long-range educational initiative without equal. It would have pleased many contemporary reformers of the educational system.

In spite of the magnitude of the effort, education barely reached the Indian peoples. The presidency of Lázaro Cárdenas, starting in 1934, implemented agrarian reforms, nationalized oil, retook the main flags of the social revolution, and modified the Constitution to give education a socialist orientation. It found the Indians in conditions of extreme misery, marginalization, and isolation. President Cárdenas decided to give them special attention.

The First Multicultural Educator of the Americas

President Cárdenas was convinced that the full and effective integration of the Indians into the life of the country was necessary and beneficial for everyone.

> Mexico is not interested in the disappearance of the Indian races and should not look for it. The government and the Revolution consider that the Indian peoples are capable, in a degree not only as high as that of the *mestizo,* but the same as any other racial type in the world. The only thing that the Indian has lacked is the possibility of instruction and nourishing like the one other peoples have had (Cárdenas 1978, 244).

What was needed was

> respect for all their values and cultural patterns, stimulating the full development of the potentialities of their race, and implying the mutual enrichment of two cultures, the Indian and the western (Loyo 1985, 451).

The backbone of his multicultural effort was education—although the term "multicultural education" had not entered the elite or the popular imagination.

"Cultural missions" were substituted for centers of Indian education. The Instituto Lingüístico de Verano, with American support, emphasized the study of Indian languages to provide multilingual education. The Department of Indian Affairs (later the National Indigenous Institute) was created to study the problems of Indian peoples emphasis on solutions and their concerted implementation. The President insisted that the new "educational agencies" should work with the whole community, *not* just the young.

The peoples' rejection of educational agencies was a continual source of concern. The teachers were often forced to call the civil and military authorities to capture the students who escaped from the educational centers of their community. But the effort was sustained; even intensified. "Penetration brigades" aspired to cover every aspect of communal life. The "agents" often felt perplexed: how to respect and revalue all aspects of Indian culture while imposing the alien values of education upon them, under the assumption that their real life was inferior in every aspect? Equally puzzling was the fact that Whites and *mestizos* had to teach the benefits of living in community to peoples who for centuries have had a community life and whose social organization was in many cases a model (Loyo 1985, 451)!

The reciprocal enrichment of Indian and western culture, continually emphasized by President Cárdenas, was synthesized into a slogan orienting the whole effort: "Our Indian problem is not to conserve the Indian as 'Indian,' neither indigenize Mexico, but to Mexicanize the Indian" (quoted in Loyo 1985, 451). There were efforts of *castellanización* (teaching Spanish), as in the old times. But bilingual education was explicitly promoted. And the model for dealing with "small nationalities" in the Soviet Union was adopted, although with original methods (Heath 1972, 110), assuming respect for the values, language, and customs of the Indians. Pluralism was not seen as a threat to national unity.

The Indian policy established by President Cárdenas saw many ups and downs, many changes in quality, intensity, and orientation during the next half century. Its main purpose, however, continued: to educate the Indian peoples for nationhood. There was intense and continual controversy about both the policy itself and the institutional practices associated with it. Repeated failures were attributed to a variety of causes or factors. The Instituto Lingüístico de Verano, for example, which made a decisive contribution to research on Indian languages and their use for literacy campaigns and bilingual education, was denounced as an American agency of cultural penetration and a factor in the dissolution of the communities and the Indian cultures. Bilingual education was the object of both celebration and critique; sometimes it was assumed to be an expression of a radical project of liberation, or even as a revolutionary tool; at other times it was seen as a political and cultural tool of domination. But the basic thrust of the Indian policy and its educational purpose was retained.

Its whole history was defined by its original orientation: extending the liberal ideal of the nineteenth century. There was never any intention of "indigenizing" Mexico—a project that perhaps could be dreamed of at the time of Mexico's founding when eighty percent of the population were Indians. But the fact is that the dominant ideology prevented anyone among the minorities from conceiving such a project; and no one among the majorities was thinking about a project of domination.

Neither were the policymakers able to conceive a pluralistic project with the Indian peoples themselves. *Education* that did not "Mexicanize" the Indians, *incorporating* them into the Mexican culture, was inconceivable. No one dared to define with any precision the content of that "Mexican culture," but its specific connotation was not confusing to anyone. To "Mexicanize" the Indians implied that the Indians should cease to be Indians; to be assimilated to the abstract categories of modern Mexico: citizen, voter, recipient, and claimant of rights . . . and all else involved in the formal and full incorporation into the western civilizational matrix.

It is not irrelevant that the initial impulse of the Indian policy adopted as a model the Soviet policy regarding "small nationalities," whose meaning and consequences can now be better appreciated. The respect assumed for the values and customs of the "other" (like the respect associated with multiculturalism) is only a formal cover-up—not always hypocritical or cynical—for culturicide.

From the first priests of the sixteenth century until today's initiatives to computerize the Indian languages for facilitating bilingualism and multiculturalism, education represents a threat of cultural extinction for the Indians. The threat became a reality for many: millions of Indians ceased to be what they were; they had no longer the supportive hammock (Esteva 1987) of their cultures; the promises of education were fulfilled for very few of them. Many Indians saw in education a path to liberation under the assumption of a *mestizaje:* the only way to escape from the discrimination, exclusion, and oppression associated with the condition of being an Indian. Even today, the term is pejorative. "Don't be an Indian" means, in ordinary conversation, "Do not be stupid, obtuse." Be it a threat or a promise, for the Indians the meaning of education was clear: to stop being what they were, to renounce their belonging, their place in the world.

The Failure of Education

We are not attempting here to talk about the cultures that died. Nine out of every ten of the Indians living in what the Spaniards called New Spain died during the first century of the colonial period. They died of hunger, smallpox, or through astonishing collective suicides. If their gods had died, how could they still continue living? What was the meaning of life then?

If nine out of every ten died, the survivors could not survive them. Over survivors fell a double stigma: the ignominious mark of being who they were, in a society denying them the freedom to be themselves; and the mark of still being who they were, of not having had the dignity of dying.

We resist talking here about what died, as we resist nostalgia and sentimentality. We resort to tradition. But we would like to escape from the shadows of the past. And we will not allow the shadows of the future to prevent us from enjoying the aliveness of the present. We want to speak about what is fully alive; of the present cultural creations of the denied civilizations—all those succeeding in crossing with dignity through colonizations and development, reacting with imagination in recent times to the crises of development. We want to speak about how "the people" at the margins and the grassroots are now steadfastly advancing in the challenge of regenerating their dreams, their arts of living and dying; how they dedicate themselves, with unusual vigor, to the creation of their new commons. We want to speak about the myths they are generating and the challenges they are confronting.

We must start with re-memberings to fully grasp what is happening. The "survivors" of the first century of colonization started their long struggle to reclaim and regenerate their commons. During the next two centuries they were unable to liberate themselves from the colonial oppression. Yet, in a very real sense, they put it at their margins: many of them were able to maintain, in their own spaces, their own forms of government, their own art of living and dying. Those spaces were called "Indian Republics" by the Spanish Crown, to allude to the degree of autonomy they had in the handling of their own affairs, in spite of the rigid rules imposed on them by the Crown—exploiting them "from the outside."

"Education" was central to the colonizing enterprise, although it was not called by this name. Scattered efforts to impose the official State language and literacy upon the Indians were clearly marginal to the main element of "education": to "civilize" the Indians out of their "barbarian" state. This goal was never reached. In spite of the formal domination of the religion and culture of the Spaniards, all over the country, it did not produce a *real* transformation of the majority of the Indians, who were still thinking, living, and dying within their own culture, which they were capable of preserving, always accommodating it to the conditions of foreign domination.

At the beginning of the nineteenth century, the political and ideological movement to get independence from Spain was fully alive and vigorous . . . among the small minority of *criollos* (people born in Nueva España from Spanish parents) and the "legitimate"[1] *mestizos* (people of mixed blood: Spaniards and Indians). For Jose Maria Morelos y Pavón, one of the heroes of the Independence, the "feeling of the nation" was to be governed by the *criollos,* who at that time represented no more than 3 percent of the population!

The Indian peoples were not included in the new political project that has now completed almost two centuries. Mexico, the fruit of an unfortunate invention, became an independent State before having constituted itself as a nation (Wolf 1958). The small, predominantly *criollo* group that conceived this State sought to use the Spanish system of domination for their own advantage and to bring to the new country they dreamed of, even by force, the institutions that were then fashionable in the countries that were a model for them.

All the ideas of a nation nourishing intellectual and political independence from Spain were themselves foreign: "Almost no one was thinking thoughts based on the Mexican realities of the moment" (González y González 1974, 92). They ignored the cultures, hopes, and aspirations of the majority of the people converted into Mexican citizens. Formally crystallized into the Constitutional Act of the Federation, approved on January 31, 1824, these ideas were reduced to fit the foreign molds of States being imitated. The Constitution alluded to the Indian peoples only once, authorizing the Congress to celebrate trade treaties with foreign countries and "Indian tribes." Its authors affirmed that they were following the path and the model of "the happy Republic of the United States of America"(CNCSRFCRS 1974, 1).

That straitjacket of imported ideas, alien to the real condition of the country, came to be considered "the root and legal foundation of the Nation, the concrete manifestation of the democratic ideals of the Mexican people, a form of government that remains valid today" (CNCSRFCRS 1974, 1). None of the later Constitutions or national projects have been able to go beyond this unfortunate invention of Mexico; recognizing at long last the basic pluralism of the country— the actual condition of the majority of its inhabitants. They continued to dedicate themselves to "forge a nation," to use Gamio's celebrated phrase, forcing reality into the imported design inscribed in the founding act, and the source of an interminable dispute.

Guillermo Bonfil identified the nature of this permanent dispute, locating it in the differences between "imaginary Mexico" and "Mexico profundo" (deep Mexico): two essentially distinct and irreconcilable forms of thinking and behaving.[2] The imaginary Mexico of the elites (educational, political, or other) embodies, promotes, and constructs the nation in the mold of Western civilization. Mexico profundo is formed by those rooted in their living Meso-Middle-American lineage: those who either do not share the Western project or assume it from a different cultural perspective (Bonfil 1996, xv–xvi).

The counterpositions between Mexicans are not only of an economic nature: between the rich and the poor, the haves and the have-nots. Neither are they confined to ideological, party, or religious affiliations or to positions regarding the political or economic "model" with which to face the peoples' predicaments. All these contradictions do exist. But it would not be possible to understand them and even less so to resolve them unless framed, as Bonfil points out, in the challenge represented by the presence of two civilizations, two different horizons of intelligibility within the same society:

> Two civilizations mean two civilizational programs, two ideal models for the society sought after, two different possible futures. Whatever decision is made about reorienting the country, whatever path is chosen to escape from the current crisis, implies a choice for one of those civilizational projects and against the other (Bonfil 1996, xv).

Prior to Bonfil, this counterposition had barely been perceived. After his death, the general adoption of his terms is frequently accompanied by a forgetting of their meanings. Such negations of the country's general and obvious reality have a variety of motives and reasons. Some are strictly ideological: the conviction of the elites that all Mexicans are irremediably inscribed in the western matrix. The inexactitude of the term (with its implicit opposition to the eastern matrix that nobody in Mexico argues for) has contributed to denying the civilizational matrix of the majority of the Mexicans. Also contributing to this is the affirmation of the *mestizaje* as a sign of national identity. The interminable mixing of blood, which makes almost all Mexicans into *mestizos,* has saved the country from dangerous obsessions about racial purity. But the generalized assumption that it deposits everyone into the same civilizing matrix and the same mythical system, has no empirical foundation.

Furthermore, the counterpositions of these two civilizations are not commonly sensed because Mexico profundo has not had a project.

Continually occupied with resistance, generally dispersed, Mexico profundo has not explicitly articulated its own project to oppose the dominant project.[3] Because of this, among other factors, it has always remained subordinated under the shadow of the national project emerging from imaginary Mexico's dominant vision.

This situation is about to end. For the first time, Mexico profundo is articulating alternatives. This comes with the growing awareness of the social majorities that the dominant project offers them no dignified place. Its unification with the global economy cannot accommodate itself to the diversity of Mexico profundo; and remaining silent is a sure formula for their own permanent destruction.[4]

Mexico profundo is made up of more than Indian peoples. Although born from them, it includes the wide majority of "the people" that constitute the nation. The minority that constitutes imaginary Mexico grows more aggressive every day. Still, Mexico profundo is giving its project an inclusive character—the bases for harmonious coexistence with a general consensus never attempted by the dominant project.

Escaping Education: Learning to Listen, Then Listening

"We were looking," said the now famous subcomandante Marcos, "for an answer to an incoherent, absurd, anachronistic situation. How was it possible that so much was in the hands of so few, and so little in the hands of so many?"

With a doctorate in education and years of university teaching in hand, Marcos, a *mestizo,* came to Chiapas in 1984 with the hope of starting a revolution. He joined a small group of Indians with a lot of political experience.

At the beginning, he teaches the Indians Mexican history. Instead of educating them, however, Marcos learns from them how to become a "part of the mountain," part of "this world of ghosts, of gods that resurrect, that take the shape of animals or things." He learns to listen.

> They have a very curious way of handling time. You don't know which time they are talking about. They can be telling you a story that could have happened a week ago, 500 years ago or when the world started. If you want to know more about those stories, they say: 'No, that is the way . . . the elders say.' The elders are their source of legitimacy for everything. In fact they are in the mountain because of their elders' commands.

The group of six—three Indians, three "mestizos"—worked and learned together in the jungle. They learned of the time of the *monterias*, when big companies took off wood from Selva Lacandona, well before the Porfiriato (by the end of nineteenth century). The Indians spoke as though present for the cutting. Young people of twenty-five or thirty years old talk and give facts perfectly coherent with the profound scholarly studies of that time in Chiapas.

> How to explain this? I told myself that it was too much of a coincidence. Later I knew that in reality that is the way in which history proceeds, the other history not written. The stories are inherited and he who inherits them makes them as his own . . . Because they do not read and write, they choose a person in the community to memorize the history of the community. If there is any problem, you consult . . . this walking book.

They did not know what was happening outside their mountains.

> But the mountain teaches you to wait. That is the virtue of the warrior, to know to wait. It is the most difficult thing to learn. It is more difficult than learning to walk, hunt or load . . . To learn to wait is the most difficult, for everyone, for Indians and *mestizos*. That is what the mountain teaches you, from the small details of waiting for an animal, the time to do something or the other . . . the mountain imposes its timetable on you. You come from the city used to administering time . . . You extend the day with a light until very late in the night, to read, to study, to make things when night falls. But not in the mountain. The mountain tells you 'until here' . . . you really enter into another world . . . another form of being . . .

Two years later, the group grew.

> We were already twelve, we could then conquer the world . . . We could eat the world as if it was an apple. We were twelve.

Eleven of them were Indians. They came then to the villages to talk. The fact that they were living in the mountains won them the villagers' respect, facilitated the talk.

> And we started to talk . . . about politics. We were telling them about . . . imperialism, the social crisis, the balance of forces . . . things that nobody understood. Neither did they. They were honest. 'Did you understand?' They replied: 'No.' You were forced to adapt yourself. They were not captives . . . They told you that they had not understood a thing . . . that you should look for another word. 'Your word is too hard, we don't understand it . . . ' And then you needed to look for other words . . . to learn to speak with the people

. . . about the Mexican history that coincided . . . with their stories of exploitation, humiliation, racism. And thus started an Indian history of Mexico.
They were appropriating their history and politics . . . They explained what is
democracy and what is authoritarianism, what is exploitation, wealth, repres-
sion. They were the ones translating their history . . . we were only spectators
. . . The villagers translated their stories in another way. It is a new word that
is old, that comes from the new mountain but that coincides with what has
been said by their elders. And so it starts to run through the mountains and
the people's support starts to be stronger. When the families of the villagers
enter the Zapatista army, they start the process of cultural contagion, forcing
us to reformulate politics, our way of seeing our own historical process, and
the historical process of the nation . . . We learned to listen. Before we had
learned to speak, too much, as all the Left do . . . at least in Latin America: its
specialty is talking, no? We learned to listen, forced to do that, because it was
a language that was not your language. It was not . . . *castilla* [Spanish] [you
needed to learn their dialect]; it has its own references, its cultural frame; they
were Others. When they alluded to something, they did not want to say the
same thing you are saying. You learned to listen with great attention . . . We
had a very square notion of reality. When we collide with reality, that square
gets very dented. Like that wheel there. And it starts to roll and to be polished
by the contact with the people. It has no relation with the beginning. Then,
when they ask: Who are you? Marxists, Leninists, Castroists, Maoists, or what?
I don't know. Really I don't know. We are . . . a hybrid, of a confrontation, of
a shock, in which, I believe fortunately, we lost . . .

That happens in parallel to this process of conspiration, clandestine, collective, which already involved thousands, entire families, men, women, children, old people. They also decided to structure themselves in autonomous
governments, in reality. Diverse communities organized themselves in a kind
of parallel government . . . collective works . . . used before for the feasts, for
drinking (there was much, much alcoholism) . . . start to be used to buy guns.

We thus came to the last period . . . 1989, 1990, 1991, part of 1992 . . .
when the Zapatista army is massified, Indianized, and becomes absolutely
contaminated by the community forms . . . the Indian cultural forms . . . The
armed forces have the work of . . . protection, but the communities do the
political direction . . . [And . . . communities] start to tell us: The people want
to fight.

We tell them: 'You are foolish, the Soviet Union fell, there is no longer a
socialist side, the Sandinistas lost the elections in Nicaragua, El Salvador signed
the peace, they are talking in Guatemala, Cuba is cornered, nobody wants
armed struggle, nobody talks about socialism, or it is a sin. Everything is now
against a revolution, even if it is not socialist.' . . . They say: 'We don't want
to know what is happening in the rest of the world. We are dying and we need
to ask the people: don't you say that we must do what the people say?' '*Pues*
. . . yes.' '*Pues* . . . then, lets go to ask.'

And they asked. And the people said yes, they wanted to fight. And they started the preparation. All during 1993. Postponing the dates: November 20, December 12, December 25, December 31.

And then starts the last phase of our story. Well, I hope that it is not the last: the one in which we now are, *pues,* the one born in January 1994 (Gilly, Marcos, and Ginzburg 1995, 131–142).

From Resistance to Liberation

On January 1, 1994, a few thousand poorly armed Indians started a rebellion in the south of Mexico.[5] Their initiative precipitated the end of the old authoritarian regime. It continues to articulate the struggles of many local groups.

No other call of the *Zapatista* movement was more successful than *Basta!, Enough!* Millions of Mexicans were activated by it, shaping their generalized discontent and their multiple affirmations into a common, dignified rejection. The movement was able to encapsulate new aspirations in a way hard to categorize. Like other guerrillas of this century, the *Zapatistas* exposed the nature of the political regime against which they were in rebellion and revealed how they were forced to prepare themselves for dying and killing in an armed uprising. In contrast with all of them, however, they showed no interest in seizing power in order to impose their own regime on everyone.

"Everything for everyone, nothing for ourselves," was not a mere slogan. It continues to be an essential part of their political conception. Like other peasant and Indian rebellions in Mexican history, the *Zapatistas* are clearly interested in reclaiming their commons and liberating themselves from the specific oppression they are suffering at the local level. At the same time, in contrast with most peasant and Indian rebellions in Mexico, they are clearly interested in the political regime that will emerge in the country as a consequence of their uprising.

Their struggle for a radically democratic regime attempts to take some of the juridical and political procedures of formal democracies (an aspiration of many Mexicans) and to combine these with their own communal political traditions: where, rather than abstract codes or laws, personal behavior and social order follow very richly specified and elaborated principles, transmitted from generation to generation; where authority commands through obedience. In their commons, the *Zapatistas* and other Mexicans seek to govern themselves autonomously, well-rooted in the space to which they belong and that belongs to them. While affirming their dignity, their hopes of flourishing, enduring according to their own cultural patterns and their own practices of the arts of living and dying, they are joining in solidarity with other Mexicans to establish radically democratic regimes where all voices are heard and respected.

Perhaps the *Zapatista* movement will soon be used to describe the postmodern nature of power (Foucault 1977). It will help to understand why a country of 90 million changed in a few months, following the initiatives of a few thousand "powerless" people who dared to declare, with all dignity in their local spaces, that the emperor had no clothes. He was naked.

Despite the global emergence of solidarity for their cause, and despite the global relevance of their message to oppressed and abused groups in every nation-state, it would be a mistake to present the *Zapatistas* as engaged in global thought. Their sense of solidarity with the marginalized, oppressed, and abused across the globe does not come with the vast baggage of some universal conception of justice. By proposing forms of self-governance following their own indigenous traditions, they are simply opening the door for others to escape the monoculture and homogeneity of the model of governance imposed by nation-states worldwide. The doors they are opening lead to the lived pluriverse, being destroyed by even the best-intentioned "global thinking" or multicultural education.

"Global Power" has no other foundation than the thinking constituted of "global statements." Global forces, in their local incarnation, were challenged by the *Zapatistas*. Local initiatives spread that challenge around the globe to address other local incarnations of those global forces, forcing the latter to recede. The "*Zapatista journal*," started by a librarian in California and disseminated through E-mail, has a local profile, used by many local people, actively putting local pressures upon the local incarnations of global *chains*. The group *Acción Zapatista,* of Austin, Texas,[6] has begun regenerating the old art of pamphleteering, while at the same time giving highly sophisticated use to state-of-the-art techniques and technologies of interneting. They are now far ahead of corporations and governments, who are investing millions of dollars in research and development to mimick what grassroots groups of this kind are doing, attempting to find ways of stopping them. There is not one single "global tool" for a "global confrontation" associated with the *Zapatistas*—although thousands of pages are being written and circulated about them, while lengths of video are now being transmitted or shared around the globe.

A few months after the uprising, Marcos confessed that the "civil society" surprised both the *Zapatistas* and Presidente Salinas. "What happened in the last ten years in Mexico, at the grassroots, while we were in the mountains?" he asked himself, he asked everyone.

The transition from resistance to the liberation of "the people," which started at the grassroots, is revealing Mexico profundo's postmodernity—in spite of globalization, development, and education. Refuseniks of development, human rights, and education seek to live. The window of Mexico profundo opens onto a very wide and complex landscape of initiatives all over the world. In the lived pluriverse, diverse peoples with *a sense of place* share a common challenge, confronting their extinction by the forces of displacement. They are the refusenik cultures—they say "No"; they refuse to die out; to be beaten; to disappear . . . They know that to survive they must drop out of the global race. If they run the race, they will drop out by dying. Why, then, not drop out in order to live and flourish? This is not necrophilia. The cultures dropping out of the education/development race are biophiliacs. They are not alone in their quest for liberation from global development and education. They have each other; their solidarities with many others similarly suffering and hoping. Radical hope is the very essence of popular movements (Lummis 1996).

The Diversity of Liberation in the Lived Pluriverse

At the grassroots, the people do not *need* to be educated or conscientized to pose their own questions:

How to protect themselves—their places, their customs, their traditions for teaching and learning—from the Outsiders' culture? the culture of schooling and education, teaching how to forget the traditional sense of place?

How to marginalize the educational system and its economy that marginalizes them?

How to drop out of the culture of dropouts? How to prevent the death of their own cultural patterns of caring for their young and their old?

How to drop out of a global race in which they are doomed to be the ones trying to "catch up" in perpetuity? 3,223 years for Mauritania, developers announce . . .

Writing of her peoples' resistance to the national alliance of education, politics, economics, and other dictators, Rigoberta Menchú notes:

> We don't celebrate Guatemalan Independence Day . . . because, in fact, it isn't a celebration for us. We consider it a ladino celebration because, well, Independence as they call it means nothing to us. It only means more grief and greater efforts not to lose our culture. Other than that it has no meaning for us at all. It is only celebrated in the schools and the people with access to schools are above all people with money. The majority of Indians have no access to primary or secondary schools. The bourgeoisie, middle-class people, celebrate it but lower down there's none of that (Menchú 1994, 205).

I, Rigoberta Menchú—An Indian Woman in Guatemala continues:

> When teachers come into the villages, they bring with them the ideas of capitalism and getting on in life. They try and impose these ideas on us. I remember that in my village there were two teachers for a while and they began teaching the people, but the children told their parents everything they were being taught at school and the parents said: 'We don't want our children to become like *ladinos.' And they made the teachers leave.* What the teacher wanted was for them to celebrate the 15th of September. They had to wear school uniforms and buy shoes. *We never buy those things for children.* They told them to put on a uniform, to disguise themselves by taking off their own clothes, their costumes, and putting on clothes of all one colour. Well, the parents didn't want their children to be turned into *ladinos* and chased the teachers out. For the Indian, it is better not to study than to become like *ladinos* (Menchú 1994, 205). (emphasis added)

The questions of resistance and liberation raised vary from place to place. The challenge of going beyond the culture of schooling and education is confronted differently from place to place. For the challenge is, in fact, conceived differently from one place to another.

The Quiché of Rigoberta Menchú's place in the highlands of Guatemala physically throw the teachers out of their communities to protect themselves from the external economy that the teachers bring with them: of uniforms, shoes, and other purchased items, destructive of the local traditions. They have their own distinct cultural patterns for making and using their own clothes. The same is true of all the other "goods" that they nourish and cherish. Made within the local economy of household and commons, these are not bought or sold. To buy them is to abandon the autonomy of the "economy of gifts."

Similarly, in Ireland, to enjoy the freedom and autonomy of their own economy, to marginalize the economy of the educators, "Alternatives to Education Campaign" challenges the Minister of Education:

Dear Minister: School has encouraged me to study hard and get my points. But when I get my points, what can I do with them? Only try to get into a college somewhere. So I leave home and head for the city. Then when I qualify, what can I do with my qualification? Only look for a job. But where I come from, nobody needs points for the work being done there, and nobody needs college qualifications either. So I end up forcibly removed from my own locality and my own people . . . May I make a suggestion then . . . for a meaningful and productive life *within their own community, and in their own locality.* In rural areas in particular, this policy would tackle the twin problems of rural depopulation and rural unemployment . . . What is the point in educating people for emigration or even migration? . . . Yours sincerely, Migrant (Molloy 1991, 21). (emphasis added)

In the *ayllu* and the *chacra* of the Quechua in the Peruvian Andes, they ingest and digest the alien culture of schooling, in order to immunize themselves against the plague. Their own methods of soil culture have taught them that the arrival of every plague, every disease, reveals to them their own weaknesses; their vulnerabilities; of their physical and cultural spaces. Rather than engage in a war to throw out the pestilence attacking their physical and cultural soils, they learn to observe the pestilence. It teaches them how to overcome their own weakness and vulnerabilities:

The official system of education . . . tries to subject the Andean peoples to the order that the West wants to impose . . . Once the installation is achieved, . . . [t]here are those who . . . are enraptured by the precepts that education has taught them. They are the devoted admirers of the West. But . . . the immense majority . . . know very well what it is all about and . . . use it only when, due to life circumstances, they need to relate with the official apparatus. They maintain alive their Andean culture and their spontaneity . . . Here in the Andes we have never been conquered by European invaders, nor are we poor or malnourished or underdeveloped; nor are we victims, nor have we been subjected, nor do we demand anything . . . For us what happens is that—just like the frost, the hail or insects sometimes visit our *chacras*—five centuries ago there appeared here suddenly a very virulent plague that has gravely damaged the life and happiness of our Andean world . . . Because in that moment our world has not known how to be sufficiently harmonized, because we were careless in the daily nurturance of harmony. Since we Andeans love the world as it is, with humility and with vigor, without fear nor laments nor resentments nor anger, we have little by little found the manner in which to re-harmonize ourselves, the manner in which to cure ourselves of this terrible plague. Each day we are recovering something of the lost harmony. Each day we are closer to our plenitude. We will be fully healthy when we will have harmonized ourselves again with all those who configure the Andean world: the *Huacas* (deities), the *Sallqas* (those of the wild) and the *runas* (people). We nurture harmony when all and each of us adjust with joy and good will to the circumstances of each moment and harmony in its turn nurtures us, making us feel at ease and cared for in each moment, full of the joy of living in community (Grillo in Apffel Marglin, forthcoming).

The Zapotecs, the Mixes, or the Chatinos accept the presence of the educational system. They go through it only to come out on the other side in order to make their own cultural path; beyond the system's pyramidal verticality in order to reclaim the horizontality of their commons.

Their own parents invested too much in creating these institutions. Eliminating them is very difficult. It is easier to work around them. Within indigenous communities in Chiapas, Indian parents send their daughters—the preservers of culture—to school as little as is essential; knowing that both "normal" or bilingual education means cultural violence, acculturation destructive of personal and collective self-esteem as Indians (Falquet 1995, 6–8).

Marcos learns from the Indians of Chiapas . . . their mountains . . . their elders who know how to use the tools of oppressors for going beyond them; to come out on the other side walking the walk of their elders; to drop out, becoming refuseniks of the global machinery manufacturing the educated, imposing their economy on the uneducated.

Dropping Out

Knowledge and Judgment—attitudes peculiar to the culture of the modern West but which nonetheless claim universal applicability—constitute the contents of cultural imperialism and of official education on a worldwide scale. The school, the college, and the university are institutions which . . . fulfill . . . the function of fashioning our youth with imperialist interests (Grillo in Apffel Marglin, forthcoming).

A great achievement of world scholarship has been the creation of a universal middle class that makes an intellectual from Puno think in a manner similar to the one from Brussels, with the difference that the one from Puno will always be a disciple of the one from Brussels, but with difficulty will he become his teacher . . . If education is the method invented to prepare the individual for systematic access to the secrets of nature, what is in crisis is not only the school, that long ago showed its irrelevance to the ideals that support its gestation and development, but also the very principles that are behind the concept of education (Rengifo in Apffel Marglin, forthcoming).

At the grassroots, people live in commons. If lost or damaged during colonization and development, the people are reclaiming, regenerating or re-creating new commons according to contemporary conditions. Their postmodern vein reveals that the people are not trying the impossible or the undesirable: going back in history.

Having experienced the modern anguish, having resisted it, struggled against it, lost countless battles, they have not lost the war. They are still themselves, rooted in their own worlds. These teach them how to learn to make new paths that go *beyond* modernity: continually healing the ruptures from their past, their elders imposed upon by education and other modern technologies.

Resisting or bypassing all the institutions and practices conceived to educate them into cultural extinction, learning in freedom, they struggle against all the institutions that privatize knowledge; reduce wisdom into knowledge stock, a commodity sold and bought by those capable of paying for it. Their wisdom is a commons; neither bought nor sold. To cherish the wisdom of their elders, the people must remain dropouts or refuseniks of the educational system.

Their freedom comes from belonging; from a sense of place—to which they belong and nurture; and which belongs to them, nurtures them. No damage of the educational system is more evident and threatening for the people at the grassroots than its effectiveness for uprooting: the successful students and the dropouts become either "itinerant professional vandals" or unprofessional vandals and transients. Their common sense, their sense of place, explains how the people reroot themselves when removed from the places of their elders.

* * *

"Education?" asks Jaime Martinez Luna, a Zapotec, a singer, an anthropologist who renounced his professional career to re-root himself in his ancestral village, his culture. He is creating some spaces here where children and young people are living as learning.
In our workshops, they learn person to person, without the verticality of the educational system, where the teacher has the knowledge and the child should receive it. Here the young learn from each other . . . the basketball patio, the forest, the work of daily life, the village in general, their mother, the work of their father, everything. Learning horizontally, very soon they see what the community does: to work in common, to have a shared tradition. They strengthen their own 'education' of real things, not of abstractions.

"This 'education' does not deny formal education for the time being. Can it put the system aside?"

Our own parents invested too much work in creating these institutions. Eliminating them is too difficult. However, our workshops change the parents. They see that their children really learn what is important for the community . . .

"How can the communities organize by themselves such activities?"

First, we are involving those who organize the communal feasts, the music band, the rituals. They have been displaced by the cultural policies of the State . . . In every community, we invite those people. When we leave, they simply continue with their experiences.

"How did you conceive this?"

We did not have a project, a plan. People who like to sing came together and started to sing everywhere. The songs themselves, and the people listening to those songs, involved us in new conversations and activities. Our "theory" is only a reflection and formalization of our practice, generated by the communities themselves.

"How to nourish awareness of the things that matter?"

We challenged academic reasoning imposed on us from the outside with one rooted in our own place . . . We do not have any order or sequence, any specific program . . . Schools absorb the children, make them receptacles. They lose the possibility of reflecting on what it means to go for the wood . . . to know the work of their parents . . . what kind of plants must be collected and harvested every season . . . This is a knowledge that the children are losing by spending time in school. For some time, the parents did not dare to say anything. "If my child is in the school, he must learn there. My own knowledge has less value every day. There is no need for me to share it with him." But times are changing. The parents are observing that what they know themselves is useful for a living; and that what the children learn in the school is useless. Their children are relearning to learn what really matters.

The most important thing is to recognize our capacity to be ourselves . . . Zapotec or Mixe or Chatino. To measure our difference not as a comparison with others, but as an awareness of our own dignity . . . our freedom, a space to have our own initiatives. What is done by the destituted, the marginalized, the exploited? To look for a space of decision, and to look for it collectively. Sometimes we fail, because of the systems of control. But sometimes we succeed (Martínez, 1992).

* * *

In San Andrés Chicahuaxtla, all the women wear beautiful *huipiles* of red and white stripes. From a distance, they may appear to the stranger to be wearing a uniform. Up close, every *huipil* reveals itself as a profoundly personal creation. Each red row is woven in its own unique pattern. Every Triqui girl becomes a woman when she weaves her first *huipil* in her own personal style. Even the common symbols are combined in ways that are exquisitely singular and particular. Whoever discovers a new design or a special way of weaving is admired by everyone in the community. Weaving together, the new skill is soon shared with all the others, preventing the festering of envy or jealousy. Their wisdom is a commons. Every skill, every creative impulse, is simultaneously personal and a part of their commons.

The *huipiles* of San Andrés offer many symbols of communal life: where the personal and the common are indivisibly constituted; the unique, peculiar, and exceptional conjugated into singular wholes. San Andrés has a mode of existence typical of thousands of communities, millions of people, everywhere. At the same time, it is the exception to any norm or rule. Far from existing in the past, as a reminiscence, as many want to see them, it is a contemporary reality that seems to have in it the embryo of an *ancient future*.

The Triquis came from very far away, carrying their difficult story here, to San Andrés Chicahuaxtla. As the outcome of a peculiar chain of events, Fausto and Marcos Sandoval created "the house that collects our path"? a communal initiative that generates surprises every day.

> Education? Well our initiative reflects our own communal ways of learning. . . . Fully aware of what our culture is, we know how to take what we need from the outside to follow our own path (Sandoval 1992).

> Art, for us, is not an object for an exhibition or a sale, that only some can have; for us, what is created is shared and belongs to the community . . . In their arguments of superiority, western culture has called our history "legend"; has converted our art into folklore; has called "custom" any juridical system practiced without physical coercion; has marginalized our language (Sandoval 1992).

> Our initiative was a great dream. We have not been able to do everything we wanted. But we continue. The inhabitants of Chicahuaxtla live with dignity. . . . Each person has land and access to everything that exists in the community. In my case, after being out of the community for many years, to study in Oaxaca and Mexico City, I took the decision of coming back, because this is

my home, here is my family, here are my roots, here I have everything (Sandoval 1992, 8–10).

They tried everything. One brother became a teacher and struggled to be assigned to a nearby community. Its isolation, the virtual absence of bureaucratic control, allowed him to introduce radical changes. The children learned the practical skills needed in the community, instead of accumulating "knowledge": a collection of alien names, "facts," and figures. By the time the authorities discovered the situation and closed the school, all the children knew enough to thrive in the community.

Fausto and Marcos started their initiative with a simple experiment. They observed that the most important feast of San Andrés, the *carnaval,* was declining: children or young people were no longer interested in participating in the traditional dances and masquerades. They organized a contest, with a few small, symbolic prizes for those best representing their traditional dances. Their success took them by surprise. More groups participated in the contest than they could have imagined. The *carnaval* was transformed. The elders and the adults now enjoy the variety offered by the young. Another unexpected consequence of these initiatives is the regeneration of the *rezanderos*[7]— a species in the process of extinction. Usually very old, they had started to become very sad people: nobody was interested in learning with them. Today they *select* the best: those who really want to learn with them. Other initiatives followed these successes: a documentation center with a singular collection of books, pamphlets, and documents; a small workshop producing cassettes and videos to catalyze debates on common predicaments for the local radio station; small agricultural experiments; their list of local intiatives proceeds with variety and daily surprises . . .

For years, the Sandovals and other families selected the teachers of the school of San Andrés as the main *cargos* (communal positions of service, culminating in the position of *presidente municipal)* of the community—assuming that they "knew" more despite their lack of experience in handling local responsibilities. Following on the heels of many disasters, communal consensus concludes today that anyone but the teachers are appropriate for the *cargos,* due to their arrogance and disregard for customs and the disposition to impose their own individual authority. One teacher, for example, forced the children to wear ties to the school, in spite of the fact that no one in San Andrés and very few in Oaxaca use a tie. Others imposed national norms, deriding local customs as nonprogressive. Every time they threw a teacher out of San Andrés, the substitute turned out to be worse. Fausto used an opportunity to translate the official curriculum into Triqui, forcing the teachers to use their own language in the classroom. Fausto observed that every time the children asked their parents something about the height of the Himalayas or about the geography of Africa for their homework, the puzzled and humiliated parents failed to be of any help. He changed the content of the curriculum, focusing on the local area. At first, the parents were really happy; for they knew every river, every hill, every place in the region, better than any book or teacher. They supported their homework with a more dignified atti- tude. Soon, however, a new question emerged: why send their chil- dren to the school, if the parents and community members know more about the curriculum? They did not stop appreciating the fact that the teachers were now recognizing and appreciating what was locally im- portant in the kitchen or the *milpa,* in the feasts or the communal assemblies. Their appreciation notwithstanding, they realized that there now seemed even less reason for "institutionalizing" their children, thereby preventing them from full participation in community life.

"My education?" answers Fausto smiling; "do you mean my *horas nalga* (arse hours)? the number of hours, months, years, I put my arse on a classroom chair?"

* * *

Luis Arévalo lives in Tepito, the vast *barrio* of downtown Mexico City. He is a shoemaker, a very good one. He worked as a foreman for a big factory, came back to Tepito and after some time, as a personal and communal initiative, he founded the Free Workshop of the Art of Shoemaking.

> Education? I think that education is really bad information. Since we were children, we were made to believe that there were *caudillos,* idols, heroes. . . . That is not true . . . Instead of learning about something called Indepen- dence and Revolution in the books and the school, we must look for our independence and make our own personal revolution, for the things we can change.

"How do people learn in your workshop?"

We don't have technicians or teachers. There are some *maestros who* really know how to make shoes. And we have young people that really want to learn. We focus on shoes: an art, not an impossible science. The *chavos* (affectionate Spanish slang for "boy") can learn that art here, if they really want to . . .

Some people come to learn even though they have another income . . . even another profession. Some of them are unemployed; others are old people. They learn how to make a living, how to keep their dignity, not to own more and more, but to enjoy their time as their own and not as their bosses' time . . . and to really live.

Here, they learn something more than making shoes . . .

"And the school?"

I think it must disappear. If the parents and all the people can live together more time, and thus become really independent, we will be able to better resist the power of money.

To start, we need to use our own hands and make with them what we want. Here, to talk about the family is to talk about the community: in a sense, they are the same thing. It is easier to rescue those that do not have a professional diploma. But in our real world, we send diplomas to the garbage (Arévalo 1992).

* * *

Fernando Díaz Enciso is a brown man, short and robust. On the street of Any Town he is indistinguishable. On the streets of Santo Domingo de los Reyes, a vast *barrio* in the South of Mexico City, it is impossible not to notice him. Here he has an invisible presence. He was a key element in its construction. He came with the first group of settlers twenty-five years ago, in what was one the biggest invasions of urban land in Latin America: in one night, 25,000 well organized people "illegally" occupied this arid, hostile land at the back of the University City, the pride of public and private developers who "modernized" Mexico City: creating specialized spaces for everything (to study, buy, sleep, work, socialize, commute . . .) interconnected by speedways. While Mexico City was suffering this reformulation and trans-mogrification, the people of Santo Domingo de los Reyes focused on putting down roots in a place they could call their own. They trans-formed a hostile piece of potentially commercial land into a home for 400,000 people. Fernando Díaz accompanied his people in their epic of creating new commons. No one will call him a leader; yet he dared to resist the authorities, sticking his neck out in their complex struggles to build their homes, to illegally bring in electricity, and other adventures needed to reclaim, nourish, and regenerate the autonomy of their commons from the authorities.

> Each group has its own way; its definitions come from daily life, not from a theory. In Mexico, we are many cultures and we must respect each other, exchange experiences, and learn from each other to defend ourselves from modernity, which crushes us in ways increasingly irrational. There must be the freedom of the communities to govern themselves, without sacrificing liberties. I think that 'community rights' does not sacrifice personal liberties: the communitarian includes the personal (Díaz 1992).

* * *

After twenty years as a postman in Mexico City, Domingo Martínez was invited by his village to the *cargo* of *presidente municipal*. Accepting this traditional honor meant that he would lose the security of his job in the institutional world. Despite two decades spent in the bureaucracy, it did not take him long to opt for the security of raising his children in his traditional commons. He became a conscious refusenik of the institutional world in order to re-member with his small village commons near Oaxaca.

Javier Solís, a young member of the Solís family has returned to his plot of land in San Pablo Etla, after three years in Mexico City and one in California. Like Domingo, the postman, returning to San Pedro El Alto, Javier is a dropout of both school *and* development . . . a conscious refusenik saying "No, thanks" at the right moment. Javier bought a yoke, reestablished his *milpa* (the sacred center of crops grown in his commons), is *topil*—the lowest *cargo* in the village—in San Pablo, plays in a rock band with four friends and is the *encabezado* (the head of the procession) at the *comparsa* (masquerade) for the celebration of the Day of the Dead, leading the preparatory activities for several months. *Milpa* is not a technical activity of producing corn for him. He is fully aware that it is, in more sense than one, anti-economic: economically speaking, it could be better to work for a salary (than be absorbed for days cultivating the *milpa)* and buy state-subsidized corn. Re-embedding himself in *agri* [soil] culture is not, for him, the attitude of a smart consumer or a smart producer. He is re-embedding by re-membering within a whole set of social relationships—which keep the economy under communal control, subordinating it to cultural patterns.

Solís, Díaz Enciso, Martínez, like the Tepitans and countless others at the grassroots, are not placing their hopes in NAFTA, the cultural identity of Mexico—if that expression has any meaning—or national political projects; they are equally not dwelling on the "problems" of Mexico City—an urban settlement that can not even be conceived as a real entity, except for authoritarian purposes (Esteva 1991). Unlike professionals, they are putting all their prodigious ingenuity and talent into the regeneration of their physical and cultural soils; those living *matrias* where they find freedom and rediscover their communal virtues.

People at the grassroots live in commons. Millions live in isolated villages, far away in the mountains, where they have learned to resist colonization and development in a thousand different ways. Millions of people also live in the heart of the big cities, or at their outskirts; in the downtowns of urban monsters like Mexico City or its periphery, in Tepito or Santo Domingo de los Reyes, where they are reclaiming and regenerating their new commons. The more creatively they regenerate their commons, the more easily they go beyond education; transforming themselves: from dropouts to refuseniks.

Waking Up: Diplomas in the Survival Kit?

Half of all the children who enter Chicago's public school system drop out before they can graduate from high school. Worldwide, three quarters of all children who register in first grade never reach the grade that the law of their country defines as a minimum (Illich 1996, 257).

The worldwide bankruptcy of the educational system offers all the evidence needed to wake up from the modern "dream of reason"; a [non]virtual nightmare for most of the people of the world. Travels to the Third World are not necessary to study this bankruptcy. Schools located a few minutes driving distance from the White House render naked the folly of following the First World's educational superhighway. From that epicenter of First World education, "savage inequalities" spread with the virulence of AIDS to any and all cultures which open themselves up to educational conversion.

Chicago's catastrophic bankruptcy mirrors the educational system's reality, replicated all over the world. South of the border, in NAFTA's Mexico, for every 100 children entering primary school, only 62 conclude it and only 53 continue their studies. Only 40 conclude secondary school (three years) and only 32 continue: 25 in college and 7 in some kind of professional training (concluded only by 2.7). Only 15 of every 100 entering college conclude it and only 11 continue. And only 2.5 complete higher education [which includes certification for the professions—legal, medical, and engineering, among others]. While nine years is the constitutional level of compulsory schooling, the national average is frozen at less than six years. The upper and middle classes, however, consume twelve to twenty years of schooling. It is an offense to mention national averages among peoples left destitute in the province of Chiapas by national or global development.

Yet, replicating the educational leadership of the North, the system south of the border also offers increasing employment to the "fixers" of the system that manufactures mass graves for those whose souls it shreds. Instead of generating shame among professionals, the problems-to-be-fixed are lucratively used for generating more business than usual. Professionals prefer not to publicly point out that the educational project is catastrophic, unjust, even apocalyptic.

Hope comes from humor. At the grassroots, we find people laugh more than those at the Center or the Top. Perhaps it is time to draw on their humor to leaven the pathos, tempering the misery and injustice perpetrated globally by education. "Education for all" is the hilarious global catechism of the World Bank, the government, the political parties, and all the disabling professions wearing the mask of care. The mask does not take long to peel off as one closely studies the recent research of experts, widely diffused by the Mexican Ministry of Education. This research establishes that three people (such as teachers, writers, janitors, secretaries, builders of schools, counselors, etc.) are needed for every seven students of any grade. Given that 70 percent of Mexicans "lack" school, 30 percent of the people must give up their useful lives to "educate" the other 70 percent—the majority of whom are doomed to drop out!!!

Common women, men, and even children—their common sense and cultural imagination not dulled by education—need no statistician to know that the "caring" slogans of international institutions or of governments seeking re-election are laughable empty promises. "Education for all?" In the 1950s, the UNESCO experts, full of the development fervor fostered by Truman in 1949, considered that the main obstacle to education in Latin America was the lack of interest in it because of the miseducated priorities of the poor and the illiterate. Ten years later, the experts were profiting from a different conclusion: the obstacle, declared the latest diagnosis, is that no Latin American state could ever meet the educational demand. Their educational budgets cannot comply with the social claims and demands for this basic human need and right that they helped to promote.

Despite the increased awareness of the damage done to peoples and places by school, the demand for schooling has not declined. Nine

out of every ten Mexicans between six and fourteen years of age attend school. With a success like that of the Coke and Pepsi promo-
tions, schoolers have created a national demand for their product.
Mexico passed from the fourth to the fifth grade in the average schooling
of Mexicans, while the government raised compulsory schooling to
nine years. There are no dog catchers in Mexico. Compulsory national education, here as in other "underdeveloped" countries, is not
an enforced constitutional right. The social and psychological pressures, effective when associated with the universalizability of the American dream, are now mere leftover customs: one of several modern
inertias of daily life.

Schooling remains, for millions of young people at the grassroots,
a ritual passage, the modern "rain dance." Increasing millions are,
however, aware that the passage is blocked. Schools are a road to
Nowhere; diplomas guarantee nothing, neither learning nor jobs; neither status nor prestige; rather than correct inequalities, they perpe-
trate them. At the same time, they are discovering other rituals or
practices that may take them more effectively toward useful work that
they can share with their parents and other members of the extended
family; toward creative and productive lives in their own contexts and
communities. These contexts are creating countless uses for their tal-
ents and skills.

Diplomas may still be in demand all over Mexico. They offer, however, little if any employment insurance. Earlier on, employers raised
school requirements for the jobs they were offering, under the illusion
of getting better workers. Having discovered, however, the low productivity of a frustrated college graduate working as a janitor, clerk,
cook, technician, or mailman, they are now reducing these requirements. The social role of diplomas to sort and shift is rapidly changing.

Years ago, some of us campaigned for legislation imposing ten years
of jail upon anyone demanding a diploma to qualify for work. In the
debates generated by these campaigns, the central conclusion was that
most students will abandon education once diplomas become an illegal currency. These debates revealed the extended awareness of the
people that schools and universities are not really places for learning
useful skills or for "socialization"—as it is called. They are principally
places for procuring diplomas, which guarantee nothing in terms of
skillfulness or hard work and responsible character yet still carry the
illusion of avoiding grim disaster.

After our failures at making diplomas illegal, we have sought to
escape them by following other routes in the exact opposite direction:

we now give diplomas to anyone learning any useful skill—especially those mastered autonomously in a matter of a few hours of study with a nonexpert. After three days in our workshops on dry latrines, for example, young people now receive a big, beautiful diploma certifying them as "Experts in Alternative Sanitation." If you cannot beat them, join them, they say. One possible route for escaping the diploma game is through its multiplication—thus widening access to those who do not want to or cannot attend school. Our three-day diplomas and other certificates offer immediate access to creative and profitable occupations. We have even received support for our endeavors from the system of "open education," created by the government for "adult learners." Students can receive certification equivalent to three or six years in a few months of study in community workshops we have participated in at the grassroots.

"What is this business of the university?"—rhetorically asked don Ricardo, a prosperous peasant of San José de Gracia, in Michoacán, a few years ago. His son, a lawyer in Mexico City, had come to visit him at the same time that we were there. Explaining his failure to get a job as a lawyer, his son was mentioning examples of friends with credentials who were driving taxis or tending stalls in Mexico City. His experiences revealed his own situation to be the rule, rather than the exception. "For twenty years," argued don Ricardo,

> the whole family sacrificed itself to give you a profession. We were proud of your success in the school. The community celebrated your prize as the best student of your generation. We were deeply satisfied with our success in offering you an opportunity for escaping from the miserable destiny of a poor peasant; for leaving our poor community. And now, twenty years after all this effort, I am receiving in just one growing season more than you can get in a year. Look at your brother. I am sure he is eating better than you. What is this business of the university?

He smiled. It was obvious to all that he was neither blaming his son, nor expressing frustration or impotence. We perceived, in fact, a certain dignity in his face, reflecting a reconsideration of his own life, of the conditions offered in his place. Lacking a diploma was no longer for him a source of shame, a deficiency. His own childhood patterns for social recognition were being reestablished; beginning to make a return and be revalued.

Don Ricardo's family story is repeated in peasant households across the country. In the early 1970s, the populist government of Luis Echeverría proudly announced a new educational system for peasants' sons. Decentralized technical schools were to train them for bringing industrial agriculture to their communities; contributing to the technical and economic revolution that the country needed.

Ten years later, more than 90 percent of the graduates of this system abandoned their communities and were working for a public agency—usually in the lowest ranks of the bureaucracy—in different parts of the country. Their peasant origin qualified them to better disseminate the practices of the Green Revolution, promoted by the Mexican government with the support of the World Bank.

But then came the Third World debt crisis. Mexico's mounting debts to the First World put petty bureaucrats off the payroll; in the middle of nowhere; abandoned by the institutions that manufactured them with brilliant promises. They were taken by surprise. More than anger or frustration, they suffered disbelief. What happened to all the promises they heard in school about their brilliant modern destiny . . . careers . . . permanent job security . . . escaping the seasonal security of peasant life?

Following a period of confusion, they woke up to the brute fact that they were not in some temporary downslope, soon to be reversed by the development economists. This was no short-run economic cloudburst after which the professional experts would put them back on the road to the promised land of development. Long before the economists recognized that the golden years of the Mexican miracle were gone forever, the people came down to earth to rely again on their common sense.

Renouncing the careers of "zootaxistas" (for *zootecnista,* zootechnician) or "peterinarians" (veterinarians for pets), many reentered the communities of their childhood. Others settled in the regions they discovered when they had careers. They "peasantized" themselves again, using whatever they learned in their bureaucratic pilgrimage which had brought them in contact with peasants of different parts of the country. Their parents' traditions helped them to create new niches, within communities or peasant organizations, applying their skills to organize all sorts of initiatives: cooperatives for the production of honey; greenhouses; set up experimental fields in communal lands to test different local varieties of corn. In some communities they attempted experiments for the regeneration of the soil all too quickly depleted after the use of agrochemicals; they also contributed to improved methods of organic agriculture . . . In the majority of cases, they began looking for and finding new places inside their communities, opening new paths beyond the bureaucratic dead ends their education had led them into.

The modern system of agriculture—the product of education and development—itself started to collapse: there were no longer budgets for agricultural experiments, for the school labs, for practices in the fields, even for books, paper, or pencils. Teachers and researchers, as well as the 18,000 students that the system had enrolled in the early 1990s, suffered paralysis and impotence for awhile, compelling them to associate themselves again with their communities. Brought down to earth from their heights of educated arrogance, for the first time since their careers were launched did they really begin to be of service to their commons. Their increasing dependence on subsistence changed the whole orientation of their endeavors. They asked the peasants how they could be of some use, instead of telling them what they must do. They used the school labs for the experiments or analyses suggested by the peasants, with materials provided by the latter, rather than applying bureaucratic instructions or waiting for budgets that never arrived. A new, promising perspective started to dawn on their professional and economic horizons.

They made, as Schumacher once put it, a good thing out of a bad thing. In suggesting this, we don't want to go any further in repeating here another modern horror story about the Green Revolution. That story, spawned by the marriage of education and development, was fed to millions. They were taught to prize education as the way of escaping the hard, wretched, and poor life of the peasant. That failed and disastrous tale, with its ecological and social devastation, is by now well documented, extensively examined and described. One would need to be very blind or very rich, very stubborn or very immoral, to keep one's eyes closed to the destructive impact of that monstrous experiment of development and education devastating soil cultures everywhere, in North and South.

Emerging Coalitions of Discontents

In the landscape of burgeoning initiatives at the grassroots, we are discovering the emergence of new coalitions of discontents. Dropouts are transforming themselves into refuseniks. The ranks of refuseniks are growing due to the accretions of nondropouts.

Among the refuseniks are *pre-institutionalized* people—those who have never been included in any institutional coverage; those never exposed to medical services or a school; those who ignored "the job market" because they never asked for a job nor were ever near the possibility of being accepted for one; those that are still without automobiles—self-moved—because they use their feet or their bicycles to move around and do not perceive a "need for transportation," even if they do occasionally ride in the decrepit local bus that takes them to the only town of their *municipio;* those who never did acquire any real dependency on the Market or the State, because they knew they could only rely upon their communities for a dignified livelihood; those that have no access to the "modern marvels" of TV or the supermarkets; those that live without access to institutional services, because they have neither "needs" nor "rights"; those never solicited to make consumer claims . . .

Those *de-institutionalized,* on the other hand, were once incorporated into the institutions of the modern economy, later becoming deprived; those who lost their jobs and see no prospect of being included ever again in any payroll; dropouts of different grades of schooling, unable to continue their studies, for economic reasons; those that lost, with their jobs, their social security rights; those who can no longer use their credit cards or closed their checking accounts after losing their source of income; those who never got the house they applied for from their union, their company, their *barrio* . . . All the peasant sons who were abandoned in the middle of nowhere in the 1980s intimately know this experience of "de-institutionalization." Their ranks are increasing every day. In 1995 alone, a million Mexicans lost their jobs—thanks to the "crisis" of globalization and development.

That "crisis" helped these two groups of discontents to start looking in other directions, nourishing new hopes. Instead of clamoring for inclusion or reinclusion, they have started to avoid the traps laid by institutional promises of security. In the midst of their frustrations and disappointments, they are finding new opportunities for freedom; new possibilities for remaining outside institutional jails. Some have already discovered creative, joyful, and independent activities after being sacked from a monotonous, underpaid job; to apply again those skills disvalued in the economic boom. Peasants deprived of their previous access to the official credit are now intercropping again, thus enriching their lives and their soils. Former managers or employees are candidly questioning themselves on how they could previously accept a future of permanent slavery to the office clock and institutional norms. There are even those who keep their diplomas a secret in worlds where an interesting stigma is attached to these. There are also those puzzling over the fact that they no longer need the medical perks of the company doctor . . .

These groups of discontents listen with particular interest to the emerging arguments about institutional counterproductivity. Refuseniks of education—bored or burned-out—share stories with victims of the other professions: those who became infertile growing bananas for agribusiness; the scores who lost their babies or got cancer once the new business, promising lots of new jobs, came into town; those who got hepatitis or AIDS in a hospital; or those who discovered, with infinite anger, that the C-section or the appendectomy they suffered was unnecessary; those wondering if the cancer treatment they took was really worth it; those that can stay at home, when they are sick, and discover that fever, rather than antibiotics, is better for healing from most infections; those who rediscover the pleasure of walking or bicycling, in their own *barrios,* after resigning from the distant job to which they were transported; those learning that they will never be able to work in what they studied or discover the obsolescence or uselessness of what they learned in the school, but are thriving in a creative occupation after a short period of apprenticeship; those escaping from obesity or prescribed diets after substituting industrial junk for real *comida;* those finding alternative solutions within the extended family to the messy condition of their divorce after three years in the hands of lawyers and litigation . . .

This collection of discontents constitutes a motley multitude of highly diverse characters. Unknown and ordinary people are joined by some famous names, Nobel Prize winners, poets, painters, deprofessionalized intellectuals of every kind. And we are sure that you have a few friends or relatives for inclusion in this list—those who laugh when they hear of "sustainable development"; or who warn their neighbors about a new threatening class of ecocratic rulers. If they share strong convictions, it is usually about what they do not want; what they are firmly opposing. And while some may be cynical, many more are festive discontents—even when they cannot share with their former colleagues what they are discovering and enjoying. Some others share a silence— a solid silence; a committed, concerned silence before events or policies that throw a shadow on their hopes. While these shadows dampen their spirits, they also foster new hopes: a renewed sense of urgency for further extending their existing coalitions.

Apart from the pre- or de-institutionalized discontents, there are refuseniks whose institutional affiliations continue in discomfort; posing for them the painful schizophrenia of daily performing at a job, while seeing through the facade of productivity it proffers to the outside world. This group of discontented refuseniks gets to be even more disparate and, therefore, difficult to classify. Often its members are accused of being hypocrites: of continuing to do what gives them grief. We are talking about disparate groups of people profoundly discontented with the market or the state as mechanisms for the social control of the means of production, the allocation of resources, or the distribution of the fruits of the collective effort. Many of them talk about injustice, inefficiency, corruption, environmental destruction, violence, selfishness, isolation . . . They are thus using the same words that any decent citizen may use to describe our present world. But they constitute a special category of people, because they do not have any hope for the reform of the present system. Some applaud the Unabomber, while others wince with the anguish suffered by those committed to Gandhian nonviolence and *satyagraha*. They do not think that any cocktail, combining specified doses of market mechanisms and State interventions, can overcome our current predicaments. They are afraid of both the failure or the success of the reforms being proposed or implemented, in Cuba or Mexico, Russia or the United States, Poland or South Africa, China or India; with any ideology or any catechism, following the inspiration of the IMF, the World Bank or the Pope, Yeltsin or Clinton, Jacques Delors or the late Jacques Cousteau, Greenpeace or the Rio crowd; they are afraid that everyone and all of these reforms will be basically counterproductive—generating the opposite of what they are looking for. Although many of them are very active, politically speaking, most of them consciously refuse to participate in any political party, any bureaucracy, any formalized structure of "power." For this reason, they are frequently classified among the "silent majority": those who are disillusioned with or marginalized by "the world as it is," but have not been able to transform their discontent into awareness and strength.

The members of this class of discontents share a firm and clear conviction of the need to establish political controls over the characteristics of industrial products and the intensity of professional services. They have arrived at this conviction taking many different paths: sadness at seeing a devastated natural environment which they earlier experienced as flourishing; anguish before the behavior of their offspring after a few years of school and TV; frustration in the face of political betrayals or corruption; anxiety experiencing increased violence and injustice; fear living as they might next to a nuclear plant similar to the one in Chernobyl or Three Mile Island; ethical confusion, before genetic engineering; simple human horror before fetal manipulation. In some of them, the recent collapse of dominant ideologies helped to foster their new awareness. A few may have started to read Schumacher, Amory Lovins, Thomas Kuhn or the Rome Club Reports; some others were able to continue their search in Goodman, Polanyi, Ellul, Kohr (1992), Gandhi, Ludwig Fleck, Iván Illich . . . Some are socialists. Others are former socialists who do not want to throw the baby out with the bath water. They love to remind us about Marx's warning that "the devaluation of the human world increases in direct relation with the increase of value in the world of things," and that the focus on useful things will bring the overproduction of useless people. They remain faithful to the ideals of justice, through the social control of the means of production and the fair distribution of the fruits of the collective effort. But they have abandoned their earlier hope in the so-called dictatorship of the proletariat, the role of revolutionary vanguards or the belief in nationalization, collectivization, or slogans like "power to the masses."

Among this motley crowd, we find honest liberals—liberated from the obsession of fighting communism after the demise of the Soviet Union—now openly recognizing that market forces are no solution. They share with former socialists a reinforced commitment to democracy, while recognizing that no democratic regime can effectively deal with the present challenges—if government continues to be about the centralized, grand-scale, bureaucratic allocation of resources, and suffrage—the carpetbagging of hopes, claims, and rights; and the economy continues to be at the center of politics and ethics. Whether socialists or liberals, they challenge the acritical idea that whatever is technically possible must be done; that any technological feat should be reproduced; that science or technology is intrinsically neutral; that progress in the quantity or the quality of social products and services can be infinite. They are thus consciously opposing the "technological imperative."

Whatever their ideological source or affiliation, these discontents resist all invitations to embrace one or another variety of "global thinking." For their disenchantment with a long line of well-known "isms" has taught them that all those

> who have 'thought globally' (and among them the most successful have been imperial governments and multinational corporations) have done so by means of simplifications too extreme and oppressive to merit the name of thought

. . . Global thinking can only do to the globe what a space satellite does to it: reduce it, make a bauble of it (Berry 1991a, 61).

They also smell that power is something different from what is usually assumed. Abandoning the myth of Kings or Party Presidents, they suspect that Power is not something that can be found in a certain place, something that certain people have, something that may be reached, taken, conquered, seized, grabbed. Rather than the illusory pursuit of Power, through peaceful or violent means, to have it or to have an influence on it, they have started to believe that power may be omnipresent, but not because it encompasses all, as authoritarian thinking believes, but because it stems from everywhere: it is constituted and flows in the form of webs of ever-changing forces. Assuming that "true statements" are not right or wrong statements, but statements through which people govern themselves and others, they are focusing their interest on the institutional regime for the production of truth— a focus that paves the way for the autonomous production of truth (Foucault, 1977).

Escaping the educated imagination in search of ordinary common sense, these discontents recognize that political limits to technological designs and professional services can only be formulated, expressed, and implemented based on free and voluntary personal initiatives and decisions, and through community agreements. Very, very gradually, their gaze has begun to shift: instead of taking "the whole of society" as a reference, they are recognizing in all such political and intellectual orientations a dangerous trap. They are suspicious of abstract thinking when it is articulated as misplaced concreteness. They prefer to concentrate their thinking, imagination, and initiatives at the local level; in their concrete spaces; in their soils. They are learning anew what it is to walk on their own feet; to trust again their own noses rather than some institutional authority. They are fully exerting the "powers of the weak" (Janeway 1980), the "power of the powerless" (Havel 1985).

They share the intuition that our generation has lost its grounding in both soil and virtue. If virtue is that shape, order, and direction of action informed by tradition, bounded by place, and qualified by choices made within the habitual reach of the actor, if it is practice mutually recognized as being good within a shared local culture which enhances the memories of place, then virtue can only flourish in local spaces, among communities of peoples who recognize each other and share ideals of self-limitation (Groeneveld, Hoinacki, Illich, and friends 1991).

The different varieties of discontents are discovering paths of return and re-memberance in their *matria,* their motherland. Migrants who come back from New York or Los Angeles do not come back to their *patria,* their fatherland; they come back to their place, their soil, their community, their *matria.* Rerooting themselves, they take creative new steps in escaping the certainties of development, progress and education; recovering their own truths—with growing confidence.

The Return of the Incarnated Intellectual

Stories of recovery and regeneration are profuse and generously abundant at the grassroots. Suffering scarcities of stories is inconceivable there. Our focus has been limited for the most part to those whose education led them not to prestigious professions, but toward the jobs of petty bureaucrats in the bloating bureaucracy of the State—on its way from underdevelopment towards development. Now we turn to stories of *deprofessionalization* for the return and recovery of *incarnated intellectuals.*

We find incarnated intellectuals mostly at the grassroots. Among the most articulate of our experiences, we have discovered some in the Peruvian Andes.[8] Proyecto Andino de Tecnologías Campesinas (PRATEC) was started by a small group of development professionals in Peru, with brilliant careers. These intellectuals were part of the first generation of non-elite Peruvians of peasant origin with access to a university education.

After several decades spent as successful professionals of development and education, they could not close their eyes to the damage and destruction done by their professions to Peruvian peasants and other common people, imposing profoundly alien western ideas and practices upon them. Deprofessionalizing themselves, they began sharing their new understanding with their colleagues and previous "clients," revealing to them the violence and counterproductivity of the epistemologies and ontologies embedded in economically developing the underdeveloped. They started reaffirming the regeneration of Andean agriculture and other traditions occurring in peasant movements throughout the country. As part of their solidarities with the people, these intellectuals began to deprofessionalize themselves; decolonizing themselves of their educated cosmovision, defined by development and other western myths; abandoning the disciplinary concepts and methods they had embraced, starting in primary school and all the way into the university.

Relearning to articulate Andean ideas and practices continues to be a part of their deprofessionalization. For the recovery of their Andean world in its own terms, they relied first on remembering their experiences within their own families and communities; reexperiencing these by joining peasants, both in their social movements and in their daily living. Clearly embedded in the daily lives and practices of their new commons, their writings and research carefully keep clear of producing "scientific knowledge."

> Science is founded on a clear separation and opposition between humans and nature and between the knowing subject and the known object. For science, culture is an exclusively human attribute and precisely the quality that makes human and nature different . . . Here [in the Andean world], conversation cannot be reduced to dialogue, to the word, as in the modern western world but rather here conversation engages us vitally: one converses with the whole body. To converse is to show oneself reciprocally, it is to share, it is to commune, it is to dance to the rhythm which at every moment corresponds to the annual cycle of life. Conversation assumes all the complication characteristic of the living world. Nothing escapes conversation. Here there is no privacy. Conversation is inseparable from nurturance. For humans, to make *chacra,* that is to grow plants, animals, soils, waters, climates, is to converse with nature. But in the Andean-Amazonian world, all, not only humans, make and nurture the *chacra,* all nurture. The human *chacra* is not only made (or nurtured) by humans, rather all, in one way or another, participate in the creation/nurturance of the human *chacra:* the sun, the moon, the stars, the mountain, the birds, the rain, the wind . . . even the frost and the hail (Grillo quoted in Appfel Marglin, forthcoming).

"Conversing with nature" is not metaphoric or symbolic. It fully assumes the nondualism of the Andean world. PRATEC rejects any and every form of commodified knowledge.

> We are a living world. We live nurturing and letting ourselves be nurtured. We live the immediacy of familiarity, of nurturance, of tenderness; we love the world as it is. Here there is no separation between man and nature. Here we do not want to transform the world: we are not a world of knowledge, we are not the world of technology. Here neither subject nor object, nor ends and means, nor abstraction belong (Appfel Marglin, forthcoming).

Like the Zapatistas in Mexico, PRATEC members reject formal political organizations which "would fetter the decentralized creative capacity required by the task of decolonization." Rerooting themselves in their own physical and cultural soils, they affirm themselves, "dispensing with having recourse to the colonial authorities, breaking with the colonial authorities, leaving them thus without function and obsolete" (Appfel Marglin, forthcoming).

Frederique Apffel Marglin, reflecting on the difference between PRATEC's deconstruction of modern western knowledge and academic postmodern critiques of modernity, observes:

> PRATEC's critique of modern western knowledge first of all is a critique of the knowledge acquired by themselves and all other educated Peruvians in schools and universities; it is therefore an autocritique or rather a process of mental decolonization. Most pertinently, that critique is made from a point of view rooted in Andean cultures. In fact PRATEC's discourse on "Cultural Affirmation" is a bifocal one since they became aware that no cultural affirmation can take place without simultaneously engaging in a process of mental decolonization. This is in part so because just about every so-called descriptive category is loaded with modern western cultural baggage. This work enables the members of PRATEC to speak of modern western knowledge from the perspective of their own world views and ways of life (1995).

The firm stance of PRATEC's members against school and education comes from seeing in the Andes its abject failures—not in the conventional terms about quality or quantity—due to the successes of Andeans in continuing to be who and what they are: resilient, complicated, subtle, and unpredictable; of a world which "continues to live as a living totality and a re-creation *in spite of the school.*"

"[I]t is clear," they note,

> that the colonizers do all that they can so that the school is substituted for the Andean way. This compulsive, fundamentalist spirit is what damages, erodes, and causes problems for the harmonious recreation of life. But its victories . . . have been momentary; they have not achieved the death of nurturing. Such that in spite of the worldwide enterprise for development and education, the Andean world is one of the most diverse on the planet . . . And in the middle of a crisis of modernity and of the educational system, both locally and worldwide, the Andean people recover their spaces (Rengifo in Appfel Marglin, forthcoming).

While delving deep into the depths of their own traditions, PRATEC's members show how they are nurtured by the ideas of Illich in their journeys of deprofessionalization. These journeys are also taking them far from home through new solidarities and networks with other Centers for Mutual Learning (CML) in several parts of the world (Apffel Marglin 1995).

To end for now our description of *incarnated intellectuals,* we briefly meditate on the life and learning of Don Fidel Palafox. His story illustrates one among many different types of recovery occurring at the grassroots; of people healing themselves from the damage of education and development. We tell his story not because it offers any paradigm for cultural recovery and regeneration. Instead, precisely because of its singularity and particularity, it offers a flavor of the diversity of initiatives we savor and enjoy in the lived pluriverse.

Don Fidel Palafox, a peasant, lives in the State of Tlaxcala, north of Mexico City, where he was born in 1895. He started to work on the land when he was fourteen years old. For more than eighty years, don Fidel Palafox nurtured the land and was nurtured by it. He spent half of his life "administering" different *haciendas,* all in the same region. As a careful and patient observer of natural processes and peasant practices, he continued to experiment with ways of improving the relationship between people and their land. Once he felt his experience was mature enough to be useful for others, he started to write down what he had learned. He was then forty years old. After his work was concluded, however, he resisted publishing it for four decades, in spite of the insistence of his friends. Finally, in 1988, presented with new pressures, he accepted publication. At ninety-eight, he had two more books ready to go to print.

We pause to reflect on the historical sequence creating these three different sets of conditions: those fostering in don Fidel the impulse for writing, those creating his resistance to publish his writings, and those finally overcoming that resistance.

Don Fidel's book is a jewel of peasant wisdom, a brief encyclopedia of placed knowledge. "Told" in simple language, through the pertinent use of local, vernacular expressions, don Fidel organizes and systematizes his lifelong observations and experiences. He describes carefully, with patience and rigor, sensible agricultural practices for the region he learned to know so well. He wrote the book in the early 1940s, just after the agrarian reform of President Cárdenas, when the people were full of hope, dreaming again their own dreams.

But then came the Green Revolution. He saw around him the invasion of alien practices and the devaluation of peasant knowledge. *Campesino,* a word symbolizing dignity, became a bad word. *Campesino* is peasant, *paysan*—a word that has had derogatory connotations for a long time. It comes from the Latin, *pagensis—ager,* the territory of a *pagus* or canton, the country. In early uses, the word *peasant* was used for foreign countries and connoted the lowest rank. It was antithetical to the noble or the prince, and also had inferential connotations of serf or villain.

Because of the development of his place, don Fidel, a wise peasant, learned that peasant knowledge, like the rest of his world, was a "leftover." He did not dare to publish his book when the very quality of his life, the treasure of wisdom he was trying to put in written words, was not only disqualified but doomed to extinction. It was publicly paraded as a straitjacket for peasants like don Fidel, a chain trapping them in their undesirable past.

But then came the Third World debt crisis, with its decade of development lost. New peasant initiatives emerged. A new ethos, beyond development and education, appeared everywhere. Peasants began revaluing their world. A peasant leader, a woman, became the Governor of Tlaxcala, the province in which don Fidel worked during his whole life.

This Governor and other friends begged don Fidel to publish the book. He finally accepted. He has refused to die before finishing his work. He knows many of us long to learn from his wisdom.

But What to Do with the Children?

Philipe Ariès (1962) and others reveal that childhood is a very recent invention. All kinds of economic and political pressures—including compulsory schooling or the legal control of so-called "child labor"—continue to be exerted upon the people, forcing them to accept the transmogrification of their offspring into childish beings.

The resistance of the social majorities to this specific form of colonization has succeeded for the most part. Their daughters and sons, nieces, nephews, and godchildren are accepted as full members of their communities rather than individuals whose childishness must be justified as a necessary feature of teens, preteens, and postteens.

At the grassroots, children are really desired, not only in emotional terms but as responsible members of the household—sharing work, obligations, and predicaments as well as opportunities for enjoyment. Far from being irrelevant or an economic burden, they constitute the very center of family life. Among peasants or marginals, the question of what to do with the children, how to entertain them, how to get rid of them, cannot even be posed or conceived. Radical differences distinguish the family life of the social majorities from that of other social classes.

Wearing the spectacles of economists and other professionals, we can objectively conclude that children are highly profitable investments for their underdeveloped parents. After the first two or three years of life (in which the mother provides most of the food needed, and other expenses for the child continue to be limited), the new member of the household and commons starts to contribute towards their sustenance. In other social classes, in contrast, "children" and young people represent a heavy "investment." Professionals we know personally bemoan the fact that, given how expensive daycare and other services have become, they have to postpone bearing a child till they can economically afford to have one.

What this economic mind hides, however, is that the "care" and "protection" of children in the modern context, in fact, disables them: represents a radical discrimination against a vast group of people, explicitly excluded for years from a robust participation in family and community life, doomed to confinement in "caring" institutions which additionally disable them (Illich and Kenneth 1977).

This situation is better understood if the size of the family is also considered. The so-called nuclear family—a creation of the economy—has already appeared in Mexico. The number of families of four or five members, like the middle classes, constantly increased in the last decades, and now represents a third of the population. Fortunately the extended family still prevails. Half of Mexican families still have more than five members; 10 percent have more than ten members. To complete this picture, it must be considered that these figures refer to the household. In both urban and rural families, several households belonging to the same family often live in the same neighborhood at the grassroots. This brings the numbers of the extended family up to several dozen. In the villages, families of 50 or 100 members, living close to each other, are far from being the exception.

Dwellers of the land still live in a commons. After all these years of expert analyses on emigration through development, the last census revealed that six out of every ten Mexicans still live in the province in which they were born. In the 1980s, the decade with the highest rate of migration between provinces, when a fifth of the population changed their place of residence, a number of them were *coming back* to their province of origin. These flows are in clear contrast with the American pattern where every person changes his/her place of residence seven times, on an average. If the figures in their coldness tell anything, they establish radical differences between developed "residents" and underdeveloped "dwellers" of the land. [Orr 1992]

Questions about what to do with the children at the grassroots cannot be conceived as problems or challengs, or, even less, as requiring imported caring institutions. Bypassing education and giving up childhood, peoples at the grassroots are not renouncing the joys and pleasures of having children; nor are they renouncing the natural human act of learning—through living and doing. Quite the opposite. Keeping alive their own cultures, regenerating their cultural spaces, they are recovering historical continuities damaged by education; they are enriching and multiplying their opportunities for learning and strengthening every form of cultural initiation.

They refuse to mimic developed peoples' goal of no demographic growth—a condition that they cannot conceive. There has been a radical change in their "reproductive patterns." The annual rate of demographic growth in Mexico fell almost to a half in the last twenty years. But it still was 2 percent in 1990, Mexican women still have an average of 2.5 children, and Mexico's population will double every thirty-five years.

In many rural villages, the first birthday is celebrated when the child is three years old. That very day, accepted as a full member of the community, the child begins participating in most community activities: births, deaths, feasts, funerals and all the regular rituals of a rich cultural life, becoming part of productive, religious, or political activities. Two out of five Mexicans are less than fourteen years old. If they were given the usual professional treatments applied to modern childhood, they would suffer severe discrimination. At the grassroots, people have successfully learned not to renounce the freedoms and opportunities for contributing to the community enjoyed by their children.

Dissolving Needs

When I was a child, more than fifty years ago, remembers Gustavo,

> the word 'needs' was only used when, for example, my mother instructed me to ask where I might 'make' them, while visiting a house where, not having been there before, we did not know the location of the latrine. Nobody would have considered a school, a health center, a book, or a telephone as a 'need.'

Twenty years ago, when a presidential precandidate was organizing Public Assemblies of Investment all over Mexico to promote his nomination, he arrived in a remote village of central Mexico. On one side, there were the officials of almost every agency, setting up their shop windows to display all the goods and services they had to offer. On the other side, there were the representatives of the communities sent to expose their "needs": potable water, credits, roads, schools, jobs

. . . the whole repertoire of petitions. Almost at the end, don Chuy spoke. "We are so poor," he said, "that we don't have any of the needs mentioned by our *compañeros*. We only want to continue living. But now they are preventing us from even that."

Almost everyone laughed at don Chuy's expression, remembers Gustavo, attributing it to the poverty of his language . . . to typical peasant ignorance. Later, in conversation with don Chuy, his vocabulary, rich in vernacular textures, revealed how his people had succeeded in preventing the development discourse from invading and polluting their perceptions; how they still possessed the words of those who have not lost their grounding in their own soil. Don Chuy's people did not have "needs": they were busy enough with living, fully aware of the restrictions imposed on the human condition. They supported their own initiatives for the most part, allowing them to flourish and endure on their own terms. For some new experiments, they were requesting a small loan. But no institution responded to their request: the loan requested was too small and failed to focus on the "needs"—basic and other—that constitute the package of development.

"Needs," in its modern meaning, did not appear with development. It emerged with capitalism and modernity, when the enclosure of the commons, in England, created the conditions for the transmogrification of humans into "needy" beings; when scarcity was established as the organizing principle of social life, disembedding the economy from the culture, and instituting it as an autonomous sphere at the center of politics and ethics.[9]

The pursuit of education and development, in the postwar era, brought "needs" to the center of the western political discourse, giving new appeal to the term. It became the educated man's word: the most appropriate to designate the moral relations between strangers in a world dreamt up of welfare states (Ignatieff 1984; Illich in Sachs 1992). The concept, hopefully, will not last much longer. It provided managers with a philanthropic rationale for the destruction of cultures. Furthermore, it is now being replaced by the new emblem of "basic requirements," under which the latest global project—"survival of the earth"—can be justified.

Since the 1970s, all the failures of development concurrently fostered new labels to renovate that myth, even when acknowledging its limits and contradictions. Paul Streeten showed that *successes* in reaching the goals of economic growth were the *cause* of hunger and misery. He thus proposed the Basic Needs Approach, as an effort parallel to development, if the conditions of the social majorities were to be improved (Streeten 1979). Given the limits to growth, identified by the Club of Rome (Meadows [and others] 1972), new campaigns were launched for giving underdeveloped peoples at least the fulfillment of their "basic needs." Manfred Max-Neef shaped in "alternative" terms his design for the "other" development (Dag Hammarsjold Foundation 1975). These orientations put aside any critical debate about development, permeating most strategies and programs ever since.

Today, it is not easy to challenge the modern premise of needs, so well rooted in the educated mind. Only a few have perceived the historicity of the present notion: the way it has transformed the perception of human nature, in the last 50 years; transmogrifying *homo sapiens* into a *needy man;* transforming a dimension which is part and parcel of the human condition—its limitations, its radical immersion in its environment—into dependence on the market economy and addiction to specific goods and services defined as "needs" (Illich 1977).

To go beyond education and development means learning to abandon the path of progress that creates "needs" where previously none existed. It means escaping the mindset of "basic needs"—including "the basic human need for education." By acknowledging the incommensurability of cultures, peoples liberated from the obsessions of education and development are able to propose their own cultural redefinitions of the good life. Any new universal formulation of "human needs" threatens the lived pluriverse of the social majorities.

No new paradigm is needed as a substitute for the needs that come with education and development. Flourishing beyond the reign or need of education, different peoples and cultures conceive incommensurable ideals of life and of social organizations in the lived pluriverse.

Grassroots Postmodernism

Postmodernism at the grassroots describes an ethos of women and men who are liberating themselves from the oppression of modern economic society. The reign of *homo educandus* and *homo oeconomicus* go hand in hand. Liberation from the one cannot occur without liberation from the other.

Learning to marginalize the economy has nothing to do with suppressing money or stopping trade. Similarly, learning to marginalize the educational system has nothing to do with stopping the all-too-natural disposition of people to learn about life and living in their contexts. It is finding cultural alternatives to the One World (Sachs 1992) of education molded to exclude all other cosmovisions except that of *homo oeconomicus* or *homo educandus.*

The political design establishing modern societies excised the economic sphere from society and culture, while installing it as an autonomous domain at the center of politics and ethics. That brutal and violent transformation, first completed in Europe, has always been associated with colonial domination in the rest of the world.

Grassroots postmodernism (Esteva & Prakash 1997) opens windows to the initiatives of people for regaining their autonomous cultural spheres from the clutches of the economy; while reembedding it (to use the expression of Polanyi 1975), subordinating it again to politics and ethics; marginalizing it—putting it at the margin—which is, precisely, what the "marginals" are doing.

But what is being marginalized at the grassroots? It is the idea of scarcity—a principle, a logic that they are marginalizing from the center of life. It is not rarity, shortage, restriction, want, insufficiency, even frugality. The sudden shortage of fresh air during a fire is not scarcity of air in the economic sense. Neither is the self-imposed frugality of a monk, the insufficiency of stamina in a boxer, the rarity of a flower, or the last reserves of wheat mentioned by the Pharaoh in what is the first known historical reference to hunger.

The "law of scarcity" was construed by economists to denote the technical assumption that man's wants are great, not to say infinite, whereas his means are limited though improvable. The assumption implies choices about the allocation of means (resources). This "fact" defines the "economic problem" *par excellence,* whose "solution" is proposed by economists through the market, the plan, or the state.

At the grassroots, we are learning what is involved in giving up that assumption. Just that. An assumption. A belief, a statement through which many people have been governing themselves and others. Marshall Sahlins (1972) and Pierre Clastres (1987), among others, have given detailed and well documented accounts of cultures in which noneconomic assumptions govern the lives of the people and which reject the assumption of scarcity whenever it appears among them.

Our experiences at the grassroots reveal to us that this is not something belonging to the past, something to remember, but a contemporary practice among the social majorities. It is the very condition for their survival. They are suffering, of course, all the damaging consequences of economic development. They are not living out of the planet that is dominated today by the economic assumptions of *homo oeconomicus.* They are fully immersed in a world daily attacked by the economic plague. They need to struggle, day after day, with the economic mind; with the economic invasion of their lives—frequently supported by bulldozers and the police, always at the service of development; with the thousand-and-one personifications of *homo oeconomicus,* surrounding and frequently attacking them. But they do find support in their own traditions, as they continue to challenge economic assumptions both in theory and practice (Esteva 1993).

When learning and knowledge are organized around the assumption of scarcity, the majority of people at the grassroots are not only deprived of the proper access to the "system" where the new commodity is kept under control by the "knowledge capitalists," the educated and their public or private bosses. Their own ways of learning are also cancelled, reduced or devalued, and their wisdom, their own relations with the world, are deprecated by the market.

Bypassing schooling and education, the people are putting into proper perspective the professional gateways, controlling who enters or exits from the centers of the economy. Some might see this as either ignorance or a case of sour grapes. We have learned to understand it as cultural autonomy.

The people are exercising the power of their cultures. These teach them not to struggle for the security proffered by these economic centers. They also see that education is not going to transport them to the upper echelons of economic society's pyramid of success.

Using their feet to walk around and beyond these, the people are keeping alive their home economics—that nurtures, nourishes, and sustains them (Berry 1987, 1990, 1992). They are recovering and protecting their own ways of teaching and learning—those that enrich and regenerate their commons and their places of dwelling—where they gain their sense of place, their common sense (Robert 1996).

Showing us how they exercise their own powers, common women and men are also teaching us how to dissolve for ourselves the "professional secrets" of educators: of "scarce" knowledge capital, bought and sold to keep the economy going; to gain or maintain institutional privilege.

The epic now evolving at the grassroots, whose beginnings we roughly sketch, teaches us what it is to live in commons beyond modernity. Or often against modernity, after escaping education.

Notes

1   Many "mestizos" were not "legitimate": they were living and dying among the Indian peoples, accepted by them, but not by the society of Spaniards, *criollos*, and "legitimate" mestizos.

2   The expression "imaginary Mexico" is unfortunate, as Bonfil himself recognized toward the end of his life; it would be more appropriate to talk about the "fictitious Mexico." Regarding the expression "deep Mexico" (Mexico profundo—the expression adopted in the English edition of the book), it has suffered a clear impoverishment in the use given to it by the media and by daily conversation. In some sectors, it is "a vague denomination of an even vaguer idea" (see Paz 1996). But Mexico profundo is a precise technical category, theoretically delimited. There exist discrepancies as to its pertinence and value, but it cannot be qualified as "vague," that is, of "indeterminate meaning or use." As a sociological and anthropological category, it can form part of a disciplined and rigorous analysis of reality and be the object of empirical studies that put its usefulness to the test. Currently, it fulfills an efficient function as the emblem of explicit political positions.

3   One of the main reasons for this lack is that a political project, in the modern sense of the word, does not come *naturally* from the vision of Mexico profundo. They cannot conceive such a system of domination.

4   For a long time, some sectors of these majorities surrendered their will to the dominant projects because of the relative "benefits" offered. They were happy enough not to be among the marginalized, who for their part did not have sufficient strength to confront simultaneously the dominant minorities and these strata of majorities who had allowed themselves to be seduced by the minorities. The ranks of the marginalized, who under the current version of the dominant project are in fact doomed to extinction, are now being strengthened by the disposed and disposable from the relatively prosperous majorities who have lost in these years a good part of the "winnings" to which they had surrendered themselves. One and the other both feel the urgency now of joining forces to react to the ever more fulfilled threats they are facing. An expression of the emerging political coalitions was evidenced on July 6, 1997, when the political opposition won the midterm elections, thus putting an end to the authoritarian regime of the last 70 years.

5   For an analysis of the postmodern Zapatista movement signaling the end of the modern era in Mexico, see Esteva 1994a,b. Also see Autonomedia 1994. For analyses of other important local movements, see Esteva & Prakash 1992, 1996, 1997 and *The Ecologist* 1992.

6   For the most complete and current publications on the *Zapatistas*, contact Zapnet collective: E-mail:zapnet@actlab.utexas.edu; web: www.actlab.utexas.edu/zapnet; mail: 3115 Tom Green, # 405/Austin, TX78705.

7   As in many other traditional villages, the *rezanderos* play a key role in San Andrés. They conduct all prayers, in the absence of priests, for every purpose, both personal and collective; in the families as well as in the church, the fields, the feasts . . . The prayers themselves are usually a rich combination of languages. They include old modified words and phrases in the Spanish of the sixteenth century, modern constructions in Spanish, and some elements of the local language. Oral traditions nourish the creativity of the *rezandero*, who introduces changes for different motives and reasons, without breaking the line of continuity that defines the tradition.

8   We met Grimaldo Rengifo in April 1992, in the Colloquium "Living with the Earth" organized by the Intercultural Institute of Montreal. We immediately became friends and since then Gustavo has corresponded with Grimaldo and exchanged materials with him and other members of his group. For the description that follows, we are using our own materials and the introduction written by Apffel Marglin, forthcoming.

9   See Dumont 1977, Esteva in Sachs 1992, Polanyi 1975, Sahlins 1972.

Part III

After Education, What?

This book is written as a celebration.

We celebrate the vitality and inventiveness of common women and men at the grassroots; the ingenuity and courage with which they survive and flourish, despite all the forms of exclusion and discrimination imposed upon them by the economy of the educated.

We celebrate the lived pluriverse of cultures that still flourish outside the monocultural educated world. They continually teach us what it means to share personal and collective knowledge in their regenerated commons; to escape the chains of commodified knowledge and skills, mass manufactured by schools and universities competing for bigger hunks of the world campus.

We celebrate the different ways common women and men practice their diverse arts of teaching and learning. Studying with them, we sense what it means to be deprofessionalized teachers and learners; to practice "peoples' science" for overcoming the expanding array of disabilities imposed by the modern professions upon their communities; for skillfully retooling their cultures, applying their traditions for changing their traditions.

We engage in this spirit of celebration with our eyes wide open to the suffering, miseries, restrictions, and threats that the social majorities endure daily. We refuse to be blind to the variety of traditional horrors that scar human communities across the world. Some of them are also succumbing to modern horrors: learned needs, demands, and expectations of the abstract institutions of national and global economies that supply goods and services to developed peoples; while controlling lives planned by planners' futures. In the villages and barrios of the social majorities, we also witness the horrors found in the suburbs and cities of the social minorities: peoples physically, mentally, and morally destroyed. Evil finds its way into human lives, disregarding the barriers of class, creed, color, or sexual orientation.

Knowing and understanding these horrors better, we join them in their call for solidarities of resistance; of liberation and autonomy from the tools, technologies, and economics of the educated. It has taken us decades to decolonize our minds; to start seeing with our own eyes; to learn how to take off the spectacles of the educated, which reduce the abundant, rich, and multitextured Two-Thirds World into the flat, bleak, space of *homo miserablis*.

Developing Education

Literacy prosecutes illiteracy . . . Blessed are those who know how neither to read nor to write because they will be called illiterate (José Bergamín, *La Cabeza a Pájaros,* quoted by Alonso 1996, 243).

[T]he major enemy . . . is . . . the fascism in us all, in our heads and in our everyday behavior, the fascism that causes us to love power, to desire the very thing that dominates and exploits us . . . The individual is the product of power. What is needed is to "de-individualize" by means of multiplication and displacement, diverse combinations. The group must not be the organic bond uniting hierarchized individuals, but a constant generator of de-individualization (Foucault 1983, xii–xiii).

At the end of World War II, the United States was a formidable productive machinery; the undisputed center of the world, the master. The United Nations Charter could not but echo the Constitution of the United States. Having won World War II, "most Americans just wanted to go to the movies and drink Coca-Cola," observed Averell Harriman, Roosevelt's special envoy to London and Moscow during the war. Their elites, however, wanted more: their new position in the world made more explicit and permanent.

On January 20, 1949, President Truman took office and launched a new era for global development:

We must embark on a bold new program for making the benefits of our scientific advances and industrial progress available for the improvement and growth of underdeveloped areas.

The old imperialism—exploitation for foreign profit—has no place in our plans. What we envisage is a program of development based on the concepts of democratic fair dealing (Truman 1949, 114–115).

By using the word *underdeveloped* for the first time in such a context, Truman changed the meaning of *development*. He created the emblem for alluding discretely or inadvertently to the era of American hegemony. Since then, most people on earth must be *educated:* learning to be developed; learning the American way of life to become full-fledged members of modern civilization.

Never before had a word been universally accepted on the very day of its political coinage. A new perception of self and other was suddenly launched globally. Two hundred years of social construction of the historical-political meaning of the term, development, were successfully usurped and transmogrified. A political and philosophical proposition of Marx, packaged American style as a struggle against communism and at the service of the hegemonic design of the United States, succeeded in permeating both the popular and intellectual mind for the rest of the century.

On January 20, 1949, two billion people became underdeveloped. In a very real sense, they ceased being what and who they were—in all their diversity. They were transmogrified into an inverted mirror of the other's reality: belittled and sent off to stand at the end of the queue; the heterogeneous and diverse social majorities reduced to the homogenizing and narrow terms of the social minorities.[2] The stage was set for global compulsory education. For the sign of identity among the developed was education.

Redefined a thousand times since 1949, global development still continues to mean that the peoples of the Two-Thirds World need to *be like them:* the developed women and men. To *learn* to be developed, the hopes and dreams of the underdeveloped must measure up to expert norms. For the professionals of developed countries already know what it is to be developed and can teach people lacking that knowledge. Their advice changed continually to amend the fabulous failures of *every* expert strategy imposed upon the masses during the four Development Decades. One advice never changed: Education.

During colonization or the first phase of their political independence, the "underdeveloped" countries were the object of diverse educational attempts. In the postwar era of global development, however, universal education became an international obsession for Right and Left, for the progressive or the reactionary.

The literate started their fullest persecution of the illiterate in all of human history. Illiterates succumbed to the literates' definitions of their deficiencies.

A Time of Renewal

The placid prosperity and conformism of the late 1940s which allowed Truman to underdevelop two billion culturally distinct peoples with his campaign, also marked the beginning of the Cold War: U.S.-style intolerance which Senator McCarthy finessed and took to new heights. That oppression propitiated relevant sectors of American political and cultural life to rediscover the American reality hidden behind the myths of affluence, equality, scientific, and artistic splendor.

Dissident intellectuals pealed off the illusions hiding mass miseries and inequalities, economic and cultural: the lack of civil liberties; authoritarianism and militarism; color, class, gender, culture, and race discrimination. Resistance flourished in diverse quarters: feminists, farmers, teachers, students, and others coalesced in common cause against the war in Vietnam. Their critical renaissance joined daily life to poetry, music, language, or clothing for expressing social ruptures from mainstream misery and violence. The American Dream is a waking nightmare—this awareness offered many a sense of renewal.

Education, one untouchable pillar undergirding the American Dream, could not but come under critical scrutiny. The educational machinery controlling Americans was nakedly displayed in Jules Henry's *Culture Against Man* (1963). His essay, "Vulnerability in Education" (1971), revealed how insecurity and dependence are used by authority to create the consensus and discipline of subordination. Scholars of school tracking studied how it solidifies the social system of castes and classes. The 1960s school critics, like their contemporary descendants in the 1990s, sought to save the project of education through radical reform.

There were exceptions. In the 1940s, Paul Goodman had started to draw the line. In the May Pamphlet of 1945, he came to the conclusion that "we draw the line in their conditions; we proceed on our conditions," if we want to extend spheres of free action until we have a free society (Goodman 1977). In the 1960s, he found himself

> rubbing elbows with people who ran things—planners, educators, jurists, senators. He did not get many ideas for educational reform by sitting on the local school board, but his new tone of voice, patiently spelling out the details, was the result of that face-to-face familiarity with his audience. He began to speak as if his program might actually be put into practice (Stoehr in Goodman 1977, xxiv).

Goodman shared with his readers some old-fashioned virtues—prudence, temperance, courage, justice—to cope with the situation. ("Coping" was in fact a word he constantly used in that period[3]).

Young people especially were outraged at how the Established Order—government, the military, industry, education, the media—connived in the abuse and disregard of every traditional value: our resources were wasted, our lovely countryside polluted, our cities a shambles; the entire network of public communications was in the service of a venal standard of living and soporific entertainment; the young were taught to behave themselves in educational salt-mines; public monies were poured into wars which destroyed other countries, or into the roads and cars which destroyed our own; young men were conscripted and sent to die in foreign lands or, if they refused, to rot in jail at home; citizens were systematically lied to about all of this, knew it, and had lost their faith in human nature, including themselves. *Goodman changed the lives of many of us simply by naming these outrages* (Stoehr, in Goodman 1977, xxv and xxvi, emphasis added).

Rejected and ridiculed in England, *Growing Up Absurd* became a best-seller at home. Goodman bought himself a suit and wrote and spoke more than before, following the principle "make hay while the sun shines"—as he later told Colin Ward. The perversions of contemporary society in general, and of the project of education in particular were fully revealed in Goodman's *Compulsory Miseducation* (1962)— the first book advocating deschooling as an alternative to the unjust, discriminatory, expensive, and inefficient educational establishment, constructed to "park" the young outside an economy which treats them as universally handicapped and useless.

The real breakthrough beyond remediation, repair, reform, and other "fix-its" came with Iván Illich's *Deschooling Society* (1970). He had already drawn attention across the world with his critique of some of society's most cherished institutions that alienate people from each other and from their traditional sources of human dignity and joy. In the late 1960s, even before *Deschooling Society*, Illich's critiques of school were already known: "The Futility of Schooling in Latin America" and "School: The Sacred Cow" (included in *Celebration of Awareness: A Call for Institutional Revolution*, published in 1971, as the first collection of his essays and articles) were the object of intense debate the very moment they appeared (1968 and 1969). *Deschooling Society*, however, brought him the acclaim and notoriety needed for his successful marginalization.

The Failure of Deschooling

As Vice-Rector of the Catholic University of Puerto Rico and member of the Board governing the whole educational system of the island in 1958, Illich came to understand how compulsory education creates structured injustice; teaching people to blame themselves for failing to reach its mirage of equality and success. Compulsory education combines the native poverty of half of the children with a new interiorized sense of guilt for failing. His conversations with Everett Reimer revealed how and why for the majority of women and men, the obligation to attend school restricts the right to learn.

During the 1960s, Illich and Reimer with Valentina Borremans, cofounder and director of the Intercultural Center for Documentation (CIDOC), organized discussions and seminars attended by John Holt, Paulo Freire, Peter Berger, José Ma. Bulnes, Joseph Fitzpatrick, Angel Quintero, Layman Allen, Fred Goodman, Gerhard Ladner, Didier Piveteau, Joel Spring, Dennis Sullivan, Everett Reimer and many others. *Deschooling Society*, an outcome of those seminars, specifically rendered tribute to two participants, who died a little later: Paul Goodman and Augusto Salazar Bondy. First published by Harper and Row in 1970, the conclusion of *Deschooling Society* was clearly and precisely presented in the introduction:

> Universal education through schooling is not feasible. It would [NOT] be more feasible if it were attempted by means of alternative institutions built on the style of present schools. Neither the new attitudes of teachers toward their pupils nor the proliferation of educational hardware or software (in classroom or bedroom), nor finally the attempt to expand the pedagogue's responsibility until it engulfs his pupils' lifetimes will deliver universal education. The current search for new educational *funnels* must be reversed into the search for their institutional inverse: educational *webs* which heighten the opportunity for each one to transform each moment of his living into one of learning, sharing, and caring. We hope to contribute concepts needed by those who conduct such counterfoil research on education—and also to those who seek alternatives to other established service industries (Illich 1970, iv–v). [Please see footnote 6 for our insertion of "not" in the second sentence of this quotation.]

Consumption, the *fundamental* function of a *schooled society*, is exquisitely learned through the ritual of schooling. Designing and packaging knowledge, schools generate the certainty that it is best acquired in graded and certificated sequences. Through its monopoly of knowledge and instruction, the school inhibits alternatives, while fostering dependence on other monopolies for goods and services. The monopolistic rituals of school merely replace those of the previous *alma mater* of western society: the church. Furthermore, like the church, the school also promotes faith in (unlimited) progress.

Why should the ritual of schooling be a precondition, a compulsory ticket for other forms of social participation? Daring to raise this question, Illich broke free of the educators' walls within which critiques of the educational system remain confined—since respectable educators, radical or other, keep clear of the danger of belling the cat or biting the hand that feeds. Free of career ambitions, autonomous of professional hierarchies, with inimitable candor and bluntness, Illich described the immoralities of the educators' economy: discriminatory in denying the competence and skills of those who do not consume credentials; akin to the Church's denial of grace or salvation to those living outside its confines. Walking with the forthright freedom of those who disestablished the hegemony of the Church, Illich uncovered the importance of liberating learning from the confines of the profession and its expanding empire. In the same vein, Goodman's reformation called for

> an upheaval of belief that is of religious depth, but that does not involve destroying the common faith, but to purge and reform it. It is evident that, at present, we are not going to give up the mass faith in scientific technology that is the religion of modern times; and yet we cannot continue with it, as it has been perverted. So, I look for a 'New Reformation.' As a corollary, I think that important agents of change will be found among professionals and academics dissenting from the establishment; and this is like the Protestant Reformation (Goodman 1969, xi).

Despite its strong appeal for industrial societies in the early 1970s, educators found it easier to misunderstand the central insight of *Deschooling Society*. Turning their backs to Illich's evidence of the educational system's counterproductivity, reformers launched a new barrage of improvements, equally counterproductive.[4]

Modern institutions, given their incumbent mythmakers' genius, have an embedded capacity to transform their failures into powerful motives for expansion. The more the failures and damages of the school are revealed, the more the funding and new resources allocated to commissions, experiments, and reforms continued to reinforce the institution. Despite the consensus Illich generated about the ills of the educational system, the professional reaction was to ask for more and better education. Ian Lister suffered "the ultimate punishment for [his] deschooling activities—being made a professor of education" (Lister in Illich 1974a, 28). His accounts of the early 1970s reveal dangers in two directions:

dangers *of* deschooling . . . [and] *to* deschooling. Deschooling argued for *structural* changes, and there were many ways of failing to achieve them: by being co-opted as add-on alternatives (the conservative pluralist approach) or by being made into fringe activities, operating at the periphery of the system. A further danger lay in encouraging the growth of alternative bureaucracies. . . . The ideas of deschooling could also become defused and diffuse through being accommodated . . . making *School Is Dead* compulsory reading on the student's book list and deschooling into fodder for courses, essays, and doctoral theses . . . career development (Ilich 1974a, 4).

Lister shares his struggles to be sure that most of his energies go in the right direction: "that is, the one that will help the human majorities, with whom deschooling has always been concerned" (Illich 1974a, 28).

Deschooling does not and cannot make any sense to the schooled imagination—of Illich's principal readers. This has been amply demonstrated already in all schooled societies. For those well tamed by the rules and laws of the educational system, Illich's conclusions bring to the surface all the fears "civilized" peoples have of the "savage" and the "wild," walking out of the familiar cave into the vast, abundant, and diverse pluriverse; where the irrelevance of school skills cannot be hidden; where schooled individual selves—units of definition, distinction and privilege in the educated world—must confront the genuine poverty of their lives, their commodified pedagogies.

This challenge continues to be too threatening for most members of the social minorities. *Deschooling Society,* if and when rarely read today, is taken by professional educators as a personal attack; a source of anguish. How can they deprofessionalize themselves, if the society itself is not turned upside down? How do they have an income? Those reading Illich feel, as Judson Jerome confessed, "furiously paralyzed"; not furious with Illich, "but at the social situation he so lucidly describes"; all too quickly concluding that "not only were (they) unlikely to attain the society he envisages . . . but even without strong desire to get there" (Jerome in Gartner et al. 1973, 104). The idea of deschooling was discussed mainly by professional educators: the experts of the social minorities. Instead of biting the hand that fed them, they offered to beautify it, taming or masking its violence.[5] All the "alternatives in education" are escape routes; rationalizing the horror revealed by Illich rather than reducing it; or easier yet, misunderstanding the main conclusions.

It is clearly preposterous to conclude that *Deschooling Society* calls for closing all schools. Even as an imaginary armchair exercise in the One-Third World, that closure reveals its impossibility. It is as crazy as taking off the tires of a car to make it run smoother and faster. The standard reading of *Deschooling Society* put the cart before the horse. His critics assumed that Illich was proposing the closure of all schools and universities as a tool for the institutional inversion of industrial society. This reading was deliberately used at times to demonstrate his proposal as unfeasible, reactionary, or plain foolishness. It also fostered counterproductive attempts to square the circle.

Cass Canfield, Harper's president, chose the book's title without recognizing its consequences for misrepresenting Illich's thoughts. The very week in which the book came out, Illich published an article advocating their *disestablishment*—which means not paying public monies for them and not granting any special social privileges to either church- or school-goers; taxing them "so that schooling becomes a luxury object and be recognized as such" (Illich in Hern 1996, viii); making illegal any social practice or ritual that creates, establishes, and anchors "in souls the myth of education," thus presenting what he still considers the main criticism of his own book (Illich in Cayley 1992, 73).

The search for alternative schools, on the other side, could have been stimulated by a critical mistake in the editions of the book.[6] Furthermore, as he later recognized, Illich called for the disestablishment of schools *for the sake of improving education.* Here lay his mistake. More important than the disestablishment of schools, Illich turned his attention to reversing those trends that make

> education a pressing need rather than a gift of gratuitous leisure.[7] I began to fear that the disestablishment of the educational church would lead to a fanatical revival of many forms of degraded, all encompassing education, making the world into a universal classroom, a global schoolhouse. The more important question became: 'Why do so many people—even ardent critics of schooling—become addicted to education, as to a drug?' (Illich in Hern 1996, viii).

In 1977, observing the ridiculous misunderstandings of *Deschooling Society,* Illich noted that his description

> of the undesirable latent functions of compulsory schools (the 'hidden curriculum' of schooling) was being abused not only by the promoters of so-called free schools but even more by schoolmasters who were anxious to transmogrify themselves into adult educators (Illich 1977, 68).

These abuses persisted, despite the fact that in mid-1971, "In Lieu of Education" (included in 1977 in his book *Toward a History of Needs),* insisted that

the alternative to the dependence of a society on its schools is not the creation of new devices to *make people learn* what experts have decided they
need to know; rather, it is the creation of a radically new relationship between
human beings and their environment. A society committed to high levels of
shared learning and personal intercourse, free yet critical, cannot exist unless
it sets pedagogically motivated constraints on its institutional and industrial
growth (Illich 1977, 68).

Professional growth by this time ensured that the educational function was "emigrating from the schools and that, increasingly, other
forms of compulsory learning would be instituted in modern society"
(Illich in Hern 1996, viii). The profession proffered this as progress.

A third stage followed Illich's queries into "the historical circumstances under which the very idea of educational needs can arise." He
came "to understand education as learning *when it takes place under the assumption of scarcity in the means which produce it*"
(Illich in Hern 1996, ix).

The parting of Freire and Illich is important for grasping this third
stage in his philosophical investigations of the substance of education. They met in the early 1960s and became close friends when
Illich accepted the tutorship of Dom Helder Cámara and was sent by
him to talk with Freire. A few years later, Illich had the opportunity to
rescue Freire from a Brazilian jail, bring him to Cuernavaca, and publish his first book out of Brazil. *Deschooling Society* refers to the
work of Freire's group with admiration.

Their parting of ways occurred when Illich moved beyond the criticism of the system of schooling. Clearly grasping what *education* does
to foster the belief that people need help or "empowerment" (as it is
called today) to "gain insights into reality, and have to be helped to
prepare for existence or for living," Illich warned of the looming threat
of today's compulsory adult education.

This became for me the thing I wanted to analyze very critically. Therefore,
despite its good and solid tradition, it was I who moved away from the approach for which Paulo has become the outstanding spokesman during the
'60s and early '70s not only in Latin America but all over the world . . . I
remember Paulo with immense affection, but also as somebody who more
and more wanted to save the credibility of educational activities at a time
when my main concern had become a questioning of the conditions which
shape education in *any* form, *including conscientizaçao* or psychoanalysis
or whatever it might be (Illich in Cayley 1992, 206–207).

In "the pedagogy of the oppressed," Illich saw another turn of the
educational screw. Neither interested in improving the educational sys-

tem nor in shutting down schools, Illich offered evidence that saying "NO" to education was a matter of decency and courage. Educational alternatives or alternative schools simply cover up the fact that the project of education is fundamentally flawed and indecent—despite its Schindlers and Schindlers' lists (Illich 1996, 258–259).

Then as now, projects to deschool *this* society are doomed. If and when schooled societies are genuinely modified for freedom and radical democracy, their educational institutions as well as their enterprise of education will crumble—organically.

Beyond Deschooling:
Education Stood on Its Head

> The great majority of all Chicago children who leave school before they graduate are . . . slum-bred. By the time they drop out they have been badly mangled in soul and body . . . But these dropouts, in another way, are also privileged because they have learned to fake almost anything, and to see the school system for what it really is: a *worldwide soul-shredder that junks the majority and burdens an elite to govern it* (Illich 1996, 258).

A few understood that Illich was not pushing for the closure of schools. Among those who did, some challenged Illich to counter the damage done by his book: the push for more efficient modes of education. Illich pondered how home education can be more efficient; consequently, more horrible.

Years later, Illich recalled this for David Cayley:

> John Holt very quickly understood. I could then give up talking about it because he took it over with his newsletter and his association. This was a beautifully monomaniacal guy, someone you occasionally went to see, just to touch him, to make certain that he did exist! And there he was with his paperclip on his shirt, strengthening his fingers for playing the cello, which he learned as a man of forty, while you talked with him, a guy who put on a green helmet when he went into the subway so he would not be disturbed and could listen to whatever recording of poetry he wanted to enjoy that day (Illich in Cayley 1992, 209–210).

The "Holt Schools," despite their name, offered resistance to compulsory education. They are not alternative schools; even less do they offer schooling at home. Rather than schooling, they offer legal protection for autonomous initiatives that go beyond education.

John Holt knew well what he was doing. Asked to define education in 1982, he replied:

It is not a word I personally use . . . Different people mean different things with it. One of its assumptions is that learning is an activity which is separate from the rest of life and done best of all when we are not doing anything else and best of all in places where nothing else is done—learning places, places especially constructed for learning. Another assumption is that education is a designed process in which some people do things to other people or get other people to do things which will presumably be for their own good. Education means that some A is doing something to somebody else B.

Pressured by the interviewer, he said:

I don't know of any definition of education that would seem to me to be acceptable. I wrote a book called *Instead of Education,* and what I mean by this title is instead of this designed process which is carried on in specially constructed places under various kinds of bribe and threat. I do not know what single word I would put [in its place]. I would talk about a process in which we become more informed, intelligent, curious, competent, skillful, aware by our interaction with the world around us, because of the mainstream of life, so to speak. In other words, I learn a great deal, but I do it in the process of living, working, playing, being with friends. There is no division in my life between learning, work, play, etc. These things are all one. I do not have a word which I could easily put in the place of 'education,' unless it might be 'living' (Falbel 1993, 13–14).

Holt realized that the standard perception of education implied some sort of "treatment." Even self-education is suggestive of a self-admin-istered treatment. Holt and Illich understood that educational treat-ments at home are a nightmare, more poisonous and dangerous than public schooling; transmogrifying parents into pseudoprofessional teachers; contaminating the natural life of the family.

Holt took further steps to heal the rupture between learning and doing created by professional educators (Holt 1965, 1972, 1974).

Not many years ago I began to play the cello. I love the instrument, spend many hours a day playing it, work hard at it, and mean someday to play it well. Most people would say that what I am doing is 'learning to play the cello.' Our language gives us no other words to say it. But these words carry into our minds the strange idea that there exist two different processes: (1) learning to play the cello; and (2) playing the cello. They imply that I will do the first until I have completed it, at which point I will stop the first process and begin the second; in short, that I will go on 'learning to play' until I 'have learned to play,' and that then I will begin 'to play.'

Of course, this is nonsense. There are not two processes, but one. We learn to do something by doing it. There is no other way. When we first do some-thing, we probably will not do it well. But if we keep on doing it, have good models to follow and helpful advice if and when we feel we need it, and always do it as well as we can, we will do it better. In time, we may do it very well. This process never ends. The finest musicians, dancers, athletes, surgeons, pilots, or whatever they may be, must constantly practice their art or craft. Every day the musicians do their scales, the dancers exercise at the barre, and so on. A surgeon I knew would from time to time, when not otherwise busy, tie knots in fine surgical gut with one hand, without looking, just to keep in practice. In that sense, people never stop 'learning to do' what they know how to do, no matter how well they do it. They must "learn" every day to do it as well as they can, or they will soon do it less well. The principal flutist of the Boston Symphony under Koussevitsky used to say, 'If I miss a day's practice, I hear the difference; if I miss two days, the conductor hears the difference; if I miss three days, the audience hears the difference' (Holt 1976, 13–14).

Instead of Education concludes with Holt's clear and precise statement: "Education—compulsory schooling, compulsory learning—is a tyranny and a crime against the human mind and spirit. Let all those escape it who can, any way they can" (Holt 1976, 222). *Growing Without Schooling,* the bulletin he published until his death, still in circulation, is full of stories about those seeking to escape education in the U.S., any way they can . . . and succeeding in the venture.

True, "refusing schools is a real possibility for everyone, which in no way limits a person's options for the future." More and more people are successfully protecting their children from that specific horror. True, "more and more voices are joining the dialogue about deschooling, as the entire system of public schooling becomes increasingly difficult to maintain" (Hern 1996, 36). But their stories illustrate how marginal their efforts remain; how successfully the educational system keeps them at its periphery.

We cannot but admire those living and swimming upstream in schooled societies. Their most difficult challenge comes probably from their experiences with deschooled children. What to do with them? The parents who are unable to put their children in the educational cage after becoming aware of its damage, find a social desert for their children outside the home and classroom. They discover themselves unable to continue with their "normal" lives, "to pay the mortgage," if their children are not in a regime of institutionalized learning. And they also find that it is almost impossible for their children to have friends and a "normal life," surrounded as they are by schooled children. If they do not want to raise their children as isolated anomalies, outsiders of the society to which they belong, they cannot "deprive" them of the school.

That is not the case among the social majorities—as we have described earlier on. Villages and *barrios,* all over the world, successfully resist the modern imposition of childhood. Their children are not
deprived of their commons—which increasingly demonstrate the re-
dundancy and counterproductivity of the educational system.

Taming the Horror:
Overcoming the Reign of Educated Literacies

There is a spiritual culture and there is another literal culture . . . Alphabet is
a false order. The alphabetic order is the biggest spiritual disorder: the disorder you can see in alphabetic dictionaries or literal, more or less encyclope-
dic, vocabularies which reveal the universal reductionism aspired to by literal
culture (José Bergamín quoted by Alonso 1996, 243).

If the popular, untutored culture disappears, so does the real poetic world.
. . . [W]ritten literature [depends] on a background of non-literary experience.
But the reverse is not true: genuine oral-popular 'literature' can exist without
literacy. If genuine oral-popular literature disappears, so too does the spiritual
life (Alonso 1996, 245).

Learning from cradle to grave under the expert instruction of the
credentialed graduate, the "civilized," literate, educated, and developed people continue to be fabulously successful in destroying linguistic diversity. With the aid of hundreds of credit hours of canned instruction, the educated of the North speak only 1 percent of the 5,000
languages that survive temporarily on earth.

Those that survive are threatened by the depredations of progress,
development, and education; by national schemes ensuring that the
masses and the classes demand education in the mother tongue, with
a smattering of bilingualism thrown in, if the State or local school
boards are amenable to such suggestions.

Different, decentralized, more hopeful stories thrive at the grassroots.

The illiterate peoples of India still enjoy their lived pluriverse of
1,682 languages—alive, spoken, untamed, and wildly variant from one
community to the next.

Twenty-three Mayan languages are still spoken in the parts of Guatemala where even the State dictatorship has failed to decimate this
existing diversity through its educational system, public or private.

In the province of Oaxaca, in Southern Mexico, where three mil-
lion live, many different cultures coexist: Amuzgos, Cuicatecos,
Chatinos, Chinantecos, Chocholtecos, Chontales, Huaves, Mixes,
Mixtecos, Nahuas, Triquis, Zapotecos, and Zoques, as well as

Afromexican communities. Each of those peoples speaks their own language and all of them have important variants. Among the Zapotecs, for example, there are clear linguistic differences among those living in the Isthmus of Tehuantepec, in the Sierra de Juárez or in the Central Valleys of Oaxaca. And there are also dialectal differences from community to community, among the more than 7,000 communities of Oaxaca. (More than 100 variants exist alone among the Zapotecs.)

In desecrated and abused Chiapas, the uneducated enjoy their Tzotzil, Tzeltal, Zoque, Chol, and Tojolabal, despite educational curricula furiously promoting Spanish.

Central America, geographically tiny, keeps 260 languages alive. In Nigeria, more than 400 languages have been counted.

> The poor in non-industrial countries all over the world are polyglot. My friend the goldsmith in Timbuktu speaks Songhay at home, listens to Bambara on the radio, devotedly and with some understanding says his prayers five times a day in Arabic, gets along in two trade languages on the Souk, converses in passable French that he picked up in the army—and none of these languages was formally taught to him. He did not set out to learn these tongues: each is one style in which he remembers a peculiar set of experiences that fits into the frame of that language (Illich in Cayley 1992, 28–29).

Similarly recounting the linguistic riches of the unlettered, Wolfgang Sachs muses over the fact that a "great number of these languages cling to remote places. They hide out in isolated mountain valleys, far-off islands, and inaccessible deserts. Others govern entire continents and connect different peoples into a larger universe" (Sachs 1992, 102); the opaque "One World" of centralized, gigantic technologies—including those of Education.

In the pluriverse of Quechua, Aymara, and other peoples in the Peruvian Andes, voices singing of resistance to the linguistic and cultural erosion of education, write of the State's Spanish culture imposed upon them through the schools and other institutions of the national economy:

> Five centuries ago there arose among us a terrible plague from whose havoc we have not totally recovered, although we are very near a complete cure . . . The plague has not taken our world away from us nor our convictions, it has not changed our way of being. Even though we often speak in Spanish . . . (Grillo in Apffel Marglin, forthcoming).

But they speak Spanish only with the outsider, Grillo, Rengifo, and other members of PRATEC tell us. With their own people, in the comfort of shared communities, among Insiders, the varying, hybrid tongues of the commons flourish, protected from the rules of expert educated grammarians and their schools, brought in all the way from Spain, where a luxurious pluriverse once flourished.

In the Iberian Peninsula, observes Andoni Alonso, a "huge variety" existed in the Spanish language during the late fifteenth century.

> At that time Spanish took different forms in Navarra, Aragón, Extremadura, Andalucía, and elsewhere, while other languages such as Basque, Galician, and Catalonian co-existed within the country. The Kingdom of Navarra, for instance, was officially bilingual, recognizing both Basque and Spanish as established languages (Alonso 1996, 244).

This linguistic pluralism was considered "natural" at the time, even by Queen Isabela, despite the *Gramatica Castellana* (Spanish grammar) dedicated to her by the grammarian Antonio de Nebrija (1444–1522).

Out of this natural "vibrant matrix," Illich's historical voyages uncover, "there gradually precipitated official languages . . . guarded in the national academies of old nations and manufactured in the language institutes of new ones" (Cayley 1992, 29). Nebrija played a critical role in one of the epochs of this history, proposing to Queen Isabela the necessity of unifying "the speech of the country to reinforce the unification of religion and political power that constituted the emergence of the modern European state" (Alonso 1996, 244).

In the same year that Columbus sailed west to his "discoveries," Nebrija proposed to Queen Isabela the importance of engineering "popular edification and administrative control" of the "loose and unruly" speech of her people. The Queen, however, "demurred on the ground that her sovereignty did not extend to the speech of her subjects who were already perfectly in command of their own tongues" (Cayley 1992, 29).

But "it was Nebrija . . . who had the future in his bones" (Cayley 1992, 29). The next logical step in this process of the modern centralization of power created education as a "need" for learning the mother tongue. Perhaps even more important than the discovery of the "New World," this emergent reality of education grounded a new political-economic order. The rest is educational history, promoting the

> certainty that children should be taught the proper forms of everyday speech, and teachers should be paid to deliver this commodity. Elements of home-grown speech recur, like weeds growing through the cracks in pavement, in the mouths of poets and dropouts, but speech that is designed, packaged, and administered predominates (Cayley 1992, 29–30).

The history of education, like the history of the modern state, tells the tale of languages and customs submerged; of communities and traditions smashed when unacceptable to the State's educators, grammarians, judiciary, and other arms of control and management. Key to progress or modernization, educators and other incumbents of the state continue to be fully implicated in the "colonization and domestication of vernacular speech by standard forms" (Cayley 1992, 28).

Yet other incumbents of these institutions—multicultural educators—are currently promising to unmask and undo the damage done to subjugate the oppressed, the colonized; to make them disappear; to reduce them to the impotence of "cultures of silence."

Despite several centuries of educational management, the uneducated social majorities are not silenced, enjoying their rich "Babel" (Panikkar 1995) of tongues in their commons. To speak with educators and other functionaries of national bureaucracies, however, they are forced to enter the world of *homo monolingus.*

Paul Goodman reminded us (long before Chomsky and other linguists) about the organic and natural ways of learning to speak—minus education:

> Kant showed that our intellectual structures come into play spontaneously, by the 'synthetic unity of apperception,' if we are attentive in real situations. They certainly seem to do so when infants learn to speak. The problem of knowing is to have attentive experience, to get people to pay attention, without cramping the unifying play of free intellectual powers. Schools are bad at this. Interesting is really good. On the other hand, according to Kant, to exercise the cognitive faculties abstractly, *ante rem*, in themselves, is precisely superstition, presumptuous theology. He wrote all this in *The Critique of Pure Reason,* which I would strongly recommend to the Harvard School of Education (Goodman 1969, 80–81).

At the grassroots, the common people live, teach, and learn their tongues, intuitively swimming with such insights. The educated continue to call their knowledge "the superstitions of the illiterate and the uneducated."

Inverting Pandora's Box

> Pandora, the All-Giver . . . an Earth goddess in prehistoric matriarchal Greece . . . let all ills escape from her amphora (pythos). But she closed the lid before Hope could escape . . .

> [The] history of modern man begins with the degradation of Pandora's myth . . . It is the history of the Promethean endeavor to forge institutions in order

to corral each of the rampant ills. It is the history of fading hope and rising
expectations (Illich 1971a, 151).

Emil Molt, the owner of the Waldorf Astoria cigarette factory of
Stuttgart, who sponsored Rudolf Steiner for founding the first Waldorf
School in 1919, wrote that the original purpose of the school was
clearly social: to provide the children of the workers and employees
the same teaching and education enjoyed by the children of rich
families.

There are now about 500 Waldorf or Steiner schools all over the
world. Some may receive State support, but most are financially self-
sufficient, receiving private support. Highly *privileged* children attend
these schools. Their parents clearly appreciate the privilege—even
though not all of them belong to the highest economic strata. Some of
them still dream of a society in which all children can attend such
schools. But even they recognize that their dream is as unfeasible today as Molt's was in his time.

Despite the prevalence of this realization among the educated, few
support Illich's twenty-five-year-old suggestion that education be heavily
taxed, along with all luxury objects that discriminate against the un-
derprivileged. Educators continue espousing radical democracy, justice, equality, and excellence as the goal of their project, while enjoying the privileges of the global educational system, designed to spew
and vomit out millions of Ds, dropouts, and failures while providing to
a few a socially recognized certificate—a *patente de corso*. This legiti-
mizes the As and other "successes" in their disposition to impose,
control and oppress, for consuming at the expense of the majorities
they doom to the life of failures.[8]

If education still has a concrete meaning, it is a conscious attempt
to turn one into "something"—Tolstoy observed. That "something" is
increasingly a specific ability to produce the "useful things" of industrial society. What is frequently forgotten, as Marx warned, is that they
want production to be limited to "useful things," but they forget that
the production of too many *useful* things results in too many *useless*
people.

We are already living in the era marking the overproduction of useless people. The Director-General of the World Labor Organization
recently declared that feeding faith in future full employment—in rich
and poor countries alike—is a most objectionable creation of false expectations. There was a time when schools operated as training
centers for industry, qualifying people for the labor market. Today, on

the contrary, they are institutional means for preventing people, as long as possible, from entering that market. The university's programmed obsolescence becomes shorter every year; and only a minority of graduates will ever find work in their field of study.

Recognizing the current predicament of the educational system, some educators feel the need to save the school by redefining its purpose (Postman 1996). Others see in *The End of School* (Leonard 1992) fresh opportunities for finding innovative teaching and learning, leading out of the contemporary institutional morass. For those weary in body and soul with "narration sickness," with the "necrophilia" of "banking education" (Freire 1993), finally there is light at the end of the dismal, dark education tunnel:

> School as we know it is doomed. And every attempt to improve—but fundamentally preserve—the present system will only prolong its death throes and add immeasurably to its costs, both financial and social. By the year 2020, if we are to survive as a democratic society, our children will have to learn in a variety of new ways, some of them already on the drawing board, some unforeseen. None of them will involve a teacher in the front of a classroom presenting information to twenty or thirty children seated in desks (Leonard 1992, 24).

Given that the "time has come to recognize that school is not the solution . . . (but) the problem," Leonard builds boldly on ideals articulated by Dewey or Freire: "The effectiveness of any learning experience," he says, "depends on the frequency, variety, quality, and intensity of the interaction of the learner." Given that fundamental fact of learning, "we must empower our educators to create interactive learning environments, rather than merely presenting information to passive students" (Leonard 1992, 26).

Leonard suggests: "Recent developments in computerized interactive multimedia can take us considerably further." He mentions George Lucas and others who show that "contemporary electronic technology, used not as an adjunct to the conventional classroom but as something entirely new, inspires cooperation, encourages learning teams, and builds student confidence . . . Moreover, this technology can join students with a whole universe of information, allowing them to reach out to other learners and teachers all across the United States and overseas and to link up with data bases that eventually will contain a goodly chunk of all human knowledge." Describing some "advanced experiences," he concludes: "The end of school could mean the beginning of an education that would tap the potential of all our children, and immeasurably increase individual fulfillment and national success as we enter a new millennium" (Leonard 1992, 28).

Five years after its publication, Leonard's article is obsolete; his technological dream a fact: multiplying millions already "communicate" and interact on the Web without the obstruction of instruction from a single schoolmaster. In fact so redundant is the familiar instructor, pedagogue, or information dispenser that there are specific instructions available for that increasingly rare moment: "when you need to contact a human." The adept surfer on the Web could learn without ever "contacting a human." [Those desperately seeking Susan and others, however, are equally free to spend most hours of their daily life "contacting humans" through the Web.] The president of IBM proudly revealed that 45 millions learned the complex skills of handling their PCs on their own or with the help of friends (on or off the Web). Neither school nor formal training was necessary.

The specter looming menacingly behind the facade of these supposedly democratizing teaching and learning technologies extends once more the iron grip of the Establishment: the "intellectual property rights regime" (one of the main battles fought in GATT-WTO); "in essence a policy by which pharmaceutical, agricultural, biogenetic, and computer software transnational companies are allowed to privatize, enclose, monopolize the cultural wealth of the planet—so that no shred of information and knowledge can 'ideally' be acquired without passing through monetary exchange, and without a toll being paid by the purchasers to these companies" (Caffentzis 1997, 15). The conglomerates of corporations and governments are trying to ensure "property rights" on each and every kind of "knowledge"—including the diverse uses of the indigenous *neem* tree, *haldi,* or *amla* used for centuries by the peoples of India to heal, enjoy well-being, or deal with termites and other "pests." "Knowledge consumers" on the Web are vying to become "knowledge capitalists," spreading information so liberally among all races, classes, and genders that they elude ATT and its 1,500,000 stakeholders.

Two contradictory analyses of the boldest, sharpest, and the best of the technological system are summarized here. On the one side, we are offered promises of perfect democracy: with access for everyone, to everything, for almost nothing. On the other side, the Orwellian concentration of money and power—totalitarian and antidemocratic. The new education/communication/teaching/learning technologies reveal the nature of economic society and its technological system—

including its educational technologies (Ellul 1964, 1980). The *illusion* of democratic access to "knowledge," hides the *reality* of its undemocratic privatization; just as the illusion of equality hides brutal injustice; or the illusion of suffrage hides the concentration of political power by a self-appointed elite; while the illusion of the "sovereignty of the consumer" hides the corporate control of peoples' lives.

State-of-the-art educational technologies of professionals driven by the prospect of new monopolies over "knowledge stock" provokes remembrance of Illich's classic metaphor for contemporary knowledge as the

> excrement of our mind which can be put together in a heap, or into places called scientific research institutions, where scientists are responsible for making it grow at a certain percentage every year. It is then marketed, channeled through the education system and consumed, incorporated, interiorized by so-called students who are really knowledge consumers or knowledge capitalists. They get knowledge stock-holding certificates (Illich in Kumar 1980, 86–87).

In the new era of information consumption, the dreaded certification analyzed by Illich may soon be redundant; its place occupied by the intellectual property rights regime in which people "are forced to pay in order to use their own knowledge. For the products now patented by transnational companies are often nothing more than 'high tech' versions of a seed, plant, organism, chemical, or drug only found naturally in the same 'low tech, low wage' country that now has to pay for it." Payments to knowledge capitalists must be made—even if the product's use "was discovered by the indigenous people of that very same country." Thus, "the unequal exchange, first defined for non-intellectual products by Arghiri Emmanuel in the '60s, could not be more complete and perverse than it is in this new form" (Caffentzis 1997, 18).

These latest modes of oppression are sparking off movements, particularly in the Third World, to halt this "conspiracy." Those movements are doomed to counterproductivity by asking, as some groups already do, for the extension of intellectual property protection to the peoples or countries whose "knowledge" is now being patented. There is no decent alternative, it seems to us, but the total and complete abrogation of all such "rights"—including the latest western obscenity of developed and educated peoples called the "protection" of life-forms.

The notion of "knowledge" implicit in the current trends increasingly involves stealing from the pluriverse of learning and knowing—

incarnated, specific, rooted, necessarily vernacular (consequently unique and diverse) forms of relationship between women and men, and between them and their living cosmos. "It is fortunate," argue the Peruvian incarnated intellectuals, "that knowledge is not pan-cultural" (Grillo in Apffel Marglin, forthcoming). And they add:

> [I]n the individualistic and highly competitive environment in which people of the modern West live, . . . the acquisition of knowledge is seen as the achievement of a highly profitable investment, as a way to build a career. [P]eople are suddenly caught involuntarily in a runaway zeal . . . in the addiction to competition for competition's sake . . . and that once in it 'one forgets to live' (Grillo in Apffel Marglin, forthcoming).

In such contexts, "love and friendship could be limitations or obstacles that hurt one's chances for career promotion" (Grillo in Apffel Marglin, forthcoming).

Reduced to a specific kind of "excrement of our minds," the knowledge of the educated continues to be a commodity, bought and sold on the market. The school was, of course, the institution that operated that reduction in a massive scale; it "educated" people to first accept and now globally market this contemporary horror.

Resistance to the universal classroom has emerged everywhere. Neo-Luddites protecting the text from its massacre by the screen are now being joined by those protecting the conventional classroom against this assault. Conventional educators argue for the old, personal relation between the teachers and the students; presenting strong and good arguments against the risks of losing "human connections" in the new scheme of things.

They are naming something that seems to them intolerable. They abhor this new twist to the economic relations that are already pervasive among and between *homo educandus*; while still idealizing education and the ideals of the educated person, failing to see that the universal classroom, now technically implemented, has inverted Pandora's myth. This inversion abandons all hope, while attempting to keep, control, or corral all human ills (Illich 1970).

Living Without Schools or Education

> Though there are machines that can work ten to a hundred times faster than man, they are not needed. The people take death seriously and do not travel far. Though they have boats and carriages, no one uses them. Though they have armor and weapons, no one displays them. [The people] return to the

knotting of rope in place of writing. Their food is plain and good, their clothes fine but simple, their homes secure; they are happy in their ways (Lao Tzu, *Tao Te Ching*).

[W]e can set the conditions for a new era in which technology would be used to make society more simple and transparent, so that all men could once again know the facts and use the tools that shape their lives. In short, we can disestablish schools or we can deschool culture (Illich 1977, 70).

Its enchantment and mystique for transforming frogs into princes and princesses now thoroughly deconstructed, the educational system continues postponing its disestablishment in the societies of the schooled and the developed; replacing *expectations* and *needs* of Promethean Man for the *hopefulness* and *sufficiency* of Pandora and her husband Epimetheus.

Illich's call for institutional inversion is echoed at the grassroots, among the illiterate social majorities, sick and tired of suffering policies promising development and progress, masterminded by educators, economists, manpower planners, and other professionals.

Meditating on the perspective of the dropouts—persons and cultures—who fail to function with the modern Rs (the Bill Gates, Apple and IBM's [un]Holy Trinity insist that these be learned on the screen), preferring their spoken words to those written[9] by the educated, we see whole worlds opening up to Illich's authentic alternatives *TO* education; *TO* schooled knowledge; *TO* the classroom; *TO* the institutionalized modes of learning and teaching destructive of the lived pluriverse.

Rendering transparent the illusions and damage perpetrated by all modern institutions—including education—Illich calls for "institutional inversion." His *Celebration of Awareness* offers an invitation to all those "unwilling to be constrained by the apparently all-determining forces and structures of the industrial age . . . of privilege and license" (Illich 1971a, 17).

Three decades ago, Illich was fully aware that his call would create major confrontations with contemporary systems. "Let us join together joyfully," he said, at the time of the March to the Pentagon, "to celebrate our awareness that we can make our life today the shape of tomorrow's future" (Illich 1971a, 18). Illich's "institutional revolution" continues to be misunderstood: associated with the seizure of power.

Seeking to understand and undertake the "institutional inversion" he calls for, we are reminded of Foucault's warning: "Do not become enamored of power"; preceded by his call:

Withdraw allegiance from the old categories of the Negative (law, limit, cas-
tration, lack, lacuna), which Western thought has so long held sacred as a
form of power and an access to reality. Prefer what is positive and multiple,
difference over uniformity, flows over unities, mobile arrangements over systems. Believe that what is productive is not sedentary but nomadic (Foucault
1983, xiii).

"Institutional inversions" are being borne by extended political coalitions of those already de-institutionalized or damaged by the institutions of industrial societies: the dropouts, the unemployed, and many
others either excluded or no longer clamoring for their re-institution-
alization. The *conditio sine qua non* of their struggle is not sour
grapes but the critical distance needed to see beyond them to better
alternatives for living as learning. While still employed by such institutions, some people are joining such coalitions for institutional inversion.

Our hope for a world beyond education rests with all the *cultures*
that have remained outside the school and other jails of the technological system (Ellul 1964, 1980); cultures that are still alive and flourishing *in spite* of the pressures, restrictions, and burdens imposed on
them by it. They protect themselves with their inbuilt barriers against
educators' assumptions of scarce means for the production and consumption of knowledge. They enjoy the affluence of living in ways
which are not disconnected from learning by doing. The cultures of
resistance and liberation do not disconnect people from the things
with which learning occurs; and neither do they dismember their communities through educators' myths of mobility.

Solidarities with the dropout cultures call for establishing *limits* to
the educational system. Their commons are protected through
marginalizing the mainstream institutions: all of which create scarcity
in every aspect of daily life. This marginalization has nothing to do
with depriving people of school; especially not those who lack the
interest or motivation to learn to survive without educational institutions. We hope, by placing limits on schooling and all the other institutions of the modern era, that those fully immersed in the institutions of the Center will in time be able to see with their own eyes the
alternatives at the margins. Those who see may then create their own
paths of liberation.

The challenge of living the good life without education is intuitively
grasped and understood by those whose common sense has not been

drowned or buried under the barrage of information prized by the proud owners of information technologies; by those who still have unschooled cultures. From them we have learned to learn without bells and bell curves, without credentials, textbooks, chalkboards, and the overwhelming perverse institutional logic that "dumbs down" all those who come under its sway. With them we have learned to free our imaginations from the clutches of classroom information; to recover our common sense before it was extinguished by underuse or denigration. For they know in their hands, their eyes, and in all their other senses what it is to learn without packaged instruction. The people at the grassroots have not forgotten the skills required to live and flourish outside the academic "cave"—with its shadows, its dark doubts that are mistaken to be liberatory or emancipatory certainties.

We celebrate in this book not only the courageous attempts of the homeschoolers and the deschoolers—going upstream in schooled societies; but, even more so the extended, massive reactions among the social majorities. True, they are ignorant of Holt's or Illich's writings and initiatives. However, their children are growing without education and have been able to translate that condition, suffered for a long time as a lack, into opportunities for the dignified and joyful regeneration of commons. It is from the unlettered and the untutored beyond the margins of mainstream institutions that we have learned to recover, remember, and reread the books that professional educators prefer to forget; that do not serve well any professional career today. Obviously, the social majorities do not read these books. They have little reason to do so. These books were not written for them. For common men and women today, as in the past, continue to enjoy the common sense, the ordinary arts of living and dying (without technological dependencies) celebrated in these books, lying in the forgotten corners of the academy.

Coalitions of refuseniks are emerging in ways that the mainstream finds more difficult to put down or to ignore as the ways of the ignorant. Illich's insights are being sensed by those who have never belonged to the Centers falling apart. Perhaps it is not incidental that Illich's reflections started in Puerto Rico: "How do you make human beings—these Puerto Rican *jibaritos* with whom I was dealing—human resources?" (Cayley 1992, 61) His work increasingly challenged what was being done to "develop" these so-called "underdeveloped" peoples. Long before his readers could comprehend him, Illich began insisting that "underdeveloped" peoples are in a better place to tame the horror—a task experienced as either impossible or an immense sacrifice by the people of the "developed" world.

> The Third World has a crucial responsibility in the liberation of the world from their idols of progress, efficiency, the GNP. Its masses are still not trapped in the habit of consuming, and specially the consumption of services. Most of the people still heal and settle and teach each other . . . The Third World could open the way in the search of a style to learn for living, a style which will be the preparation of men for satisfying authentic needs in a genuinely human context. No doubt, those nations could illuminate the way for a world as developed as it is decadent (Illich 1974b, 45).

Next to the frustrating experiences of deschoolers in the North are the different ventures of the social majorities, revealing to themselves and to others their growing new awareness of the road to nowhere built by the schooled. Before being "fully developed"—that is, before becoming fully "institutionalized," educated, empowered, or con-scientized—they are seeing through the myths of development that their own Third World political and intellectual elites are imposing upon them through forging multinational and international alliances, increasingly obsessed with catching up (as Illich predicted) rather than trying alternatives to Truman's project of global development.

The initiatives now being taken by the people at the grassroots are opposing, first and foremost, those elites. They are turning a bad thing into a good thing: using their marginalization as the context for creating new opportunities; transforming their conditions as the desperate, the passive left-overs, the dropouts, into becoming active and creative refuseniks; transforming their unfulfillable demand for education and other economic goods and services into a new awareness of the false promises of development or progress. They are recognizing and celebrating the reliability of their own traditions to achieve their cultural ideals of a good life.

We would not describe what is happening at the grassroots as the deschooling of society. Of course, sharing the hopes of the people in their struggles to protect their new commons through extended coalitions, we also nourish the hope of reaching that point where there will occur the inversion of all the oppressive institutions. We join those who also hope that in the new era, schools will become a relic of times past; monuments of a dark age examined with an archeological gaze by scholars studying the rise and fall of modernity.

Marginalized by the educational establishment and the industrial world as the ravings of a crank, Illich's wisdom already has immediate practical uses in the "marginal" world: the Two-Thirds World seeking to protect itself from its continued exploitation by the One-Third world. For Illich observes that

> [a] deschooled society . . . would rely on the autonomous and self-adjusting use of components and tools. It would encourage trust in personal experience and the rise of transitory and dispersed associations in which decisions are made by those directly affected, and in which common purpose frequently emerges only in the very instance of its achievement. Access to information and tools must be random, if new connections are to be discovered.

> If a society uses technology to increase the autonomy of each person, it follows that only procedural rules can be planned. These rules will set limits, but they leave substantive goals unpredictable. Only certain tools can be made generally available, but how they can be used cannot be predetermined.

Illich adds:

> To plan for unpredictable results is a scandal to the educator, a threat to the economist, a danger to the politician, and folly to the civil servant. The educator derives his income from the commercialization of knowledge; the economist rests his case on the possibility of measuring all values; the politician wants his power backed up by welfare institutions; the employee of national and international development agencies cannot bear to admit that he has been leading the poor down the garden path. Yet the planners are finding it increasingly difficult to live with their own predictions, which often point to disaster.

> The alternative to the present educational system and the societies it engenders is a return of responsibility for each man's present to him and to the member of the informal group emerging around him. This is an admittedly surprising proposition, but without surprise there is no hope (Illich 1971b, 10–11).

These words, written in 1971, are useful for understanding what is *actually* happening at the grassroots today. In 1992, reacting to the Earth Summit, the editors of *The Ecologist* described what the people were doing at the grassroots. All over the world, they found successful initiatives for reclaiming their commons. Their book, *Whose Common Future?* (1993), is a hope-filled, rigorous, and detailed account of grassroots initiatives undertaken by deschooled cultures. Their undertakings reflect many of the elements Illich celebrates; and, not surprisingly, they are producing in educators, economists, politicians, and civil servants the kind of reactions he predicted.

Since the 1970s, the ideas and texts of Illich have a way of reappearing—particularly at those times when the continual crisis of the educational system goes through explosions demanding urgent attention. His main conclusions about the situation and functions of the school system, a source of scandal in the late 1960s and the 1970s, then considered too radical, are now part of conventional wisdom. Even the fashionable, nonmarginal Alvin Toffler declared:

> In the economy of the third wave, education becomes something permanent, compulsive, and is integrated in the costs for the operation of business. There is no way to escape it. But I must say that *we should try to blow up our entire educational system* (I don't like hyperbolic expressions, but I cannot avoid one for this case). In fact, the educational system is but a subsystem immersed in another system that integrates the family, TV, the school, sport training . . . and the most important part, that part for which nobody has found the name (Toffler 1992, emphasis added).

The expanding educational industry of the 1990s, selling every variety of medicine or cure—radical, alternative, ecological, conventional, "back to the basics," or on the technological forefront of the cyberspace World Campus—proves that in the increasingly developed North, the immediate "inversion" of institutions that Illich hoped for in the 1970s will be postponed to usher in more educational expansion . . . mass information or nuclear technologies . . .

> the epoch of a global schoolhouse that would be distinguishable only in name from a global madhouse or a global prison, in which education, correction, and adjustment became synonymous . . . [with] new and fearsome educational devices that teach about a world which progressively becomes more opaque and forbidding (Illich 1977, 70).

Margins and Centers:
Escaping the Mythopoesis of Education

Students are not the only ones graded and ranked for their good or bad behavior, their obedience or failure to obey the norms of the Open Society's educational system. Scholars and scholarship are similarly ranked: following the same exact criteria. Underlying the creation of Centers and Margins, these criteria separate those who are certified as able or exemplary from those who are failed and ousted. All those who pose a genuine threat to the reigning "certainties," the academy's

Tower of Truths, must be sent off to the doghouse—denied jobs, tenure, or promotion; or tolerated enough to be misunderstood and misclassified: as interesting and even original thinkers whose ideas belong to "utopia" and not to the practical realities of the real world.

Despite this treatment, several survive. Against all institutional odds, their books are republished: like those of Gandhi, Iván Illich, Paul Goodman, John Holt . . . to name a smattering. Irrelevant or outdated at the centers of the academy, they offer much to the marginal; to people at the grassroots looking both for precedents and inspiration for their current endeavors; seeking articulation or solid intellectual foundations for their hopes and initiatives.

Those marginalized by Centers of academic scholarship and institutionalized knowledge are proving to be particularly pertinent for those experiencing puzzlement and perplexities in their struggle for dignity and liberation. To understand contemporary methods of marginalization, we cannot find a better case than that of Gandhi—whose myth of being much celebrated and revered hides the reality of being little read, little heard, martyred, and misunderstood.

Only a while ago, a kind and gentle editor of America's leading journal of professional education told us that our article on Gandhi's *Nai Talim* (often translated as New Education) could not be published since there was no possibility for applying his philosophy of teaching and learning in contemporary America. This recent rejection of Gandhi reminded us of not-so-recent rejections of Illich. As early as 1973, prominent educational reformers like B. Frank Brown, the Chairman of the US National Commission on the Reform of Secondary Education, declared: "Deschooling may be a useful exercise in scholarly discourse, but it cannot be taken seriously" (Brown quoted by Lister in Illich 1974a, 2).

Those committed to progress and development cannot take Gandhi or Illich seriously. Gandhi's treatment by modern India is even more instructive than his treatment in the American academy. It offers a fascinating archetype for fathoming how Centers (especially in the democratic, Open Societies of our day) systematically push all serious debunkers or challengers to their margins . . . oftentimes by placing them in seats of real importance. Modern India elevates Gandhi to the stature of saint as well as the "Father of the Nation." Standing erect on this pedestal, he is exquisitely castrated: saintliness takes him out of the running in matters practical; while fatherhood—particularly the father who is aged or elderly—reduces him down to size, to one who is not sufficiently "fast," "smart," or "with-it" to merit serious consideration in the context of modernization. Ashis Nandy reveals the intimate enemies (Nandy 1981) of Gandhi:

> Indian statists of both the right and the left have never acknowledged their enormous debt to Mr. Nathuram Godse for imposing on the Father of the Nation a premature martyrdom that straightaway gave him a saintly status and effectively finished him off as a live political presence (Nandy 1996, 2).

Crafty Gandhi, however, even half a century after his death, resists being neutered. "Their brain children still hold it against Gandhi that he has refused to oblige them and has defied the saintliness imposed on him as a strategic means of neutralizing him." No matter how weak remains the Gandhi of the Indian State and Indian nationalism, or the Gandhi of the Gandhians, the mythic Gandhi rises from the ashes; "derived from the principles of Gandhiism as they have spread throughout the world as a new legend or epic." Half a century after his assassination, he remains potent. Neither spreading a specific catechism nor a learned discourse, he remains a continual source of inspiration; constantly regenerated as "a symbol of defiance of hollow tyrants and bureaucratic authoritarianism backed by the power of the State and modern technology" (Nandy 1996, 2, 6).

Gandhism at the grassroots is not always associated with the initiatives that follow his footsteps. More often than not, the people actively practicing *satyagraha* have neither heard that word nor read Gandhi. Nonviolently, in small Gandhian ways, Gandhi's thought and praxis affects peoples' initiatives at the grassroots. Despite the educational system with which India continues aping its supposedly ousted colonizers, Gandhi's *Nai Talim* remains a presence; a celebration of the indigenous cultures of India; of agri[soil]-culture and homespun with which, despite their violent hanging-on, Gandhi spun out the last Global Empire.

Gandhi's *Nai Talim* refuses to be confined to any classroom—not even those created in Gandhian schools. It is found anywhere and everywhere, resisting the new temples of modern India: World Bank funded dams for progress and development, nuclear reactors, Miss World pageants, the State's endless schemes for deforestation, for patenting the indigenous *haldi, amla,* and *neem* . . . the list is as long as the horrors perpetrated by the best educated Indians: whose international credentials give them the legitimacy to transmogrify Truman's "underdeveloped" nation into what the developed and the developing call one of four Asian Tigers.

Incarnated Intellectuals

Like Pandora and her husband Epimetheus, the people at the grassroots are teachers of hope, humility, and sufficiency; of abandoning the arrogance of controlling the future; of practicing the arts of teaching and learning which occur organically in the context of living on soil, well rooted in soil-cultures.

We are learning from them what it means to offer our offspring as many opportunities as we can to learn with us; drawing from our ancient, rich traditions in taking our first steps toward creating our own new commons. They teach us how to commit ourselves to our immediate world; in our relations with each other and our natural spaces; in the dignity of our modest lives. Our teachers are generous in sharing with us their predicaments, the constant struggle for protection from the economic invasion of our lives. They are also generous in sharing with us the thousand and one opportunities for enjoyment—free of scarcity, indeed abundantly available in our well rooted present.

Who will educate the educators? Marx's question has no other answer but the dominant ideology, the system. Liberation cannot come from translating the "something" of education into a "political conscience" obtained through "conscientization." Who will educate the educator, the teacher-student and student-teacher?

Political awareness for escaping the tyranny of *homo educandus* and *homo oeconomicus* comes, we are learning, from the uneducated, by radically liberating ourselves from addiction to any form of education . . . to start living free of the traps of the educated conscience. We hope others may enjoy this liberation. We hope others can extend the political coalitions by which peoples' new commons are protected from the daily encroachments of the economy of education and development; and the privilege and license that inevitably arrive with them.

Bypassing the school system, people at the grassroots are applying to that modern ritual the same treatment they are creating for all the meddlesome bureaucratic procedures imposed upon them. In the new commons, people do not subordinate living to education. We are learning from them the types of damage done by separating learning from living. We now know that institutional certification produces nothing other than facilitating our relations with the institutional world.

Some of us hope that the school system will collapse, taking with it its inherent contradictions and counterproductivity. Some of us think that our societies can no longer afford to dedicate a vast proportion of their peoples to an enterprise generating inequalities, discrimination, and the loss of dignity. But we are also increasingly aware of the magnitude of professional interests and prejudices constantly reinforcing the educational system. Is there any possibility of finding attentive listeners among the million members of the gargantuan Teacher's Union in Mexico, marching year after year to demand salary increments? True, some of them are already finding their way out of the morass of the school. But how do we dissolve the social belief that education is a basic human good, a right?

Less and less do we desire to expend our energy persuading others of the moral conclusions entailed by the worldwide damage done by the educational enterprise. Instead, we are increasingly drawn to share with the dropouts—who represent the majority among us—our admiration, our new discovery of the blessings they enjoy; affirming their stance of being refuseniks. Liberating learning from education and schooling, healing from Health Care, reembedding food in agriculture, repossessing the damaged arts of dwelling, finding useful and creative work that offers cures from the addiction to jobs through creative occupation—all of these offer a perennial source of enjoyment and autonomy, radically regenerating the ancient arts of suffering and dying.

The "new social movements" and the new incarnations of the "civil society," now the object of increasing academic and political interest, are nourishing hopes at the margins and alarms at the centers. To understand these, we have found it important to study the generation of educated refuseniks who have, in the course of the last fifteen years, become members of grassroots communities. They must not be confused with the small, enlightened, dissident vanguards who emerged in the 1960s and 1970s. Unlike the latter, the former exemplify a new kind of rooted, regenerated awareness.

This new awareness, explored in the entire course of this book, is not a spontaneous product of people's Resistance. It comes with the transformation of discontents into refuseniks: those engaged in the radical reconceptualization of certainties promoted by the dominant ideologies. For their *incarnation,* they have had to do more than take a critical *academic* distance from the modern, western concepts and tools, imposed through colonization and development. More importantly, it has been necessary for them to put their feet again on real soil; to escape the mental magma now dominating the public discourse—in the think tanks, the centers for higher education and research, as well as in the popular media.

This magma is the symbolic fallout of modern technology, shaping the perception of the middle and upper classes of the One-Thirds world. Their reality, personal and collective, is increasingly shaped by an empty collection of words and statements. The invasion of plastic words (Pörksen 1995) is now superseded by "conversation" and "talk" which no longer alludes to anything real; a subsystem of the system of virtual reality.[10] This nonreality shapes the selves immersed in the dominant discourse. Media, professionals, and politicians incessantly repeat hollow catchwords and empty statements about social and personal goals. Presented as processes of democratization, these perpetuate the opposite: technical "problems" and "solutions" which create the illusion of participation in the important decisions of personal and social life, when the nation-state itself also becomes a kind of symbolic magma (Guehenno 1995).

Incarnated intellectuals are learning how to emerge out of this standardized magma of virtual reality in and through their connections with the common men and women who have never been immersed in it. Dissatisfied with the packaged knowledge manufactured by oppressive professional institutions, a few educated peoples have been searching for alternative paths. Some of them have found in their deprofessionalization unexpected opportunities for creative living among uneducated peoples—especially those successful in protecting their commons from institutionalization and its magma of virtual reality.

Drawing upon our earlier examples of incarnated intellectuals, here we take further steps in clarifying the nature of their deprofessionalization at the grassroots. It involves, first and foremost, sharing professional knowledge with the "clients" or "consumers" supposedly being served by the services of the experts. This attitude has a long tradition: of lawyers sharing legal "secrets" to avoid litigation, making themselves redundant; or of doctors explaining medical "secrets" that liberate their "clients" from expensive and unnecessary calls. Practices that lessen the control over their clientele by the professions should not be confused with deprofessionalization. Most particularly it is to be distinguished from the now standard practice of professionals, corporations, or governments which delegate to their "consumers" the functions previously performed by them, imposing "shadow work" (Illich 1981) upon their "clients": patients trained to examine their bodies or minds to facilitate the work of the medical doctors; taxpayers trained by the IRS to facilitate its control; consumer-students trained to be "enlightened consumers" of goods and services, knowing their "rights" and legal responsibilities for making lucrative claims, etc.

Departing from the gamut of practices that insert professional goods and services even deeper into the lives of people, creating stronger addictions, deprofessionalization transforms "expert-client" relationships in ways which enhance social capacities, rendering redundant the reign of "professional expertise." This behavior clearly militates against the interest of the professions for increased economic and other power. Instead, deprofessionalization puts the profession aside for the good of commons and communities; celebrating the personal autonomy and social capacities that thrive through the marginalization of the economy and its professional hierarchies.

Other facets of deprofessionalization, usually overlapping with the first, include taking distance from the language and categories which define each profession. Used to befuddle rather than profess to the public, the "technical" languages of the profession erode the public life that constitutes radical democracy (Prakash 1994). Deprofessionalizing themselves, distancing themselves from their coded practices, we know gynecologists who refuse to "deliver" babies. They render redundant the medicalization of birth by rejecting their profession's control of the natural activity of giving birth. Celebrating centuries old wisdom, gathered by women, these gynecologists "collude" with midwives in sharing the rituals of labor as natural processes rather than medical functions. Abandoning their addiction to exorbitant professional medical fees for delivery (best yet, C-sections), they stand ready to support common women—if and when called; and, they report to us, they are almost never called.

Similarly, deprofessionalized lawyers share with the people their experiences for avoiding debilitating debacles with the law. This is the clear opposite of the expertise that, for a fee, finds loopholes for avoiding taxes—a new profession in modern businesses; or transforms justice into a technical game and a soap opera—as the dream team of lawyers for O. J. Simpson has shown.

Deprofessionalized lawyers share their technical knowledge of the juridical system for finding escapes from it—ways by which the people themselves can find just ways to resolve their conflicts without recourse to the exorbitant legal system of courts, lawyers, and judges.

When deprofessionalized women and men become fully incorporated in the life of their commons—whether in rural villages or urban neighborhoods, ghettos and *barrios*—they are all too often and understandably accepted by their own people as the traditional wise women and men or the elders. Their moral and spiritual leadership lacks professional authority or power. Their specific competence articulates in new ways a shared communal wisdom. They live well by combining literate and empirical knowledge, bookish insights, and traditional wisdom—producing the *empirical knowledge of the struggle* (Foucault 1977). They perform the critical functions of facilitating processes that generate the shared communal wisdom of their common struggle. They have the "disinterestedness" in not reducing this wisdom to an individual endowment, a "knowledge capital" which promotes the benefits of the career. They understand that their own articulations are the outcomes of many shared conversations and experiences—the living interaction of different systems of knowledge, of diverse cosmovisions.

Incarnated intellectuals are differentiated from both armchair intellectuals or organic intellectuals (in the tradition of Gramsci), whose thinking and practices clearly belong to the world of abstraction and ideology. Subcomandante Marcos reveals how his own ideology—an ideology that brought him to Chiapas as an armchair intellectual in the process of becoming an organic intellectual—was dissolved in the course of his lived interactions with the Indian peoples. He is no longer what he was. He can no longer think the way he thought. He clearly contributed to a collective process that we now know as *zapatismo*. The outcome does not belong to him. But neither is he irrelevant. It was, and continues to be, a shared daily creation, profoundly and deeply rooted in the traditional soils and toils of the people.

Contemporary Prophets

For the modern mind, prophets are people who, allegedly inspired by God, can predict the future. Moderns have lost the original meaning of the word "prophet," with its allusions to women and men who gaze at the present with the lucidity needed to render opaque predicaments into fully transparent ones. With the light they shed on the present, it is possible to see clearly. Traditionally, prophets neither predict nor anticipate the future. They do not conduct cheap tours to some promised land.

At the grassroots, among deprofessionalized men and women and incarnated intellectuals, contemporary prophets profess only the possible or probable outcomes evidenced and emerging in the present.

They unveil what is hidden and rendered opaque by economic, technological, and other systems. These prophets include Gandhi, Ellul, Illich, Orwell, Berry, and others prescient of the damage contemporary institutions and technologies are doing to people and cultures, to the environment, to the human condition. Theirs clearly is the case of the road not taken; for it offers radical divergences from the superhighway's high-speed dramas and horrors. Unheeded by those racing at high speed to the top, these prophets write and speak for those ready to slow down and live (Sachs 1997, Illich 1997).

At the Centers, their hopes are scoffed as the fantasies of those impractical or deluded. Their awareness has done little or nothing to wake up the Centers. Spurning Gandhi's *Hind Swaraj,* the highly educated elite of India opted for a nation state. Instead of nonviolence and bread labor, India got management, corruption, centralization, pollution the bomb, and other forms of unlimited violence—cultural and environmental. Yet, at the grassroots, reincarnated Gandhi nourishes the awareness we are celebrating in this book.

We would not describe Iván Illich as a role model for anyone. His own condition, as a pilgrim, with no place on Earth that he can call a home, is an inverted mirror of the convivial, rooted life about which he writes. But his personal story clearly reveals how his destiny transformed him into a prophet.

As a half-Jew in the 1930s in Central Europe, he was radically uprooted. He knew at the early age of twelve that he would not bring a son to his ancestral home—breaking the tradition of centuries that was no longer present. Thus started his pilgrimage. He chose not to react to this loss with modern denial—forgetting his roots, escaping to the future, as too many contemporary men and women do, willingly collaborating with their own uprooting. Neither did he fall into nostalgia—transforming his memories into sentimentalism. Instead, he kept fully alive, in his heart, the treasure of his roots. He became consciously traditional; well anchored in his tradition, continually enriching that tradition through his historical explorations, refusing to be an accomplice to the forces uprooting him. The more he nourished his roots in tradition, the more his writings appeared to his modern readers as a fantastic *novelty.* The more deeply he entered his tradition, the more he distilled his traditional knowledge to become a flame in the darkness of modern perceptions, the more he appeared as a radical innovator.

Rooted in his tradition while rigorously avoiding any form of nostal-gia, Illich's radical innovations systematically explode any illusory bridge that takes us back in history. Instead, they open to those who gaze with him, to the surprise with which the present presents itself. Illich exemplifies the courage needed to gaze into the darkness of the present, revealing its horrors to be even worse than what he witnessed in the occupation of his place by the Nazis.

> In 1971, when I began to write *Tools for Conviviality*, on the multidimen-sional thresholds beyond which human endeavor becomes destructive of a human mode of existence, I broke down. It was the only time in my life that something which is probably called a 'depression' has hit me very deeply. I don't think I would have gone on writing if I had a son of my own flesh in my arms. I would have had to join the rain dance (Illich in Cayley 1992, 281–282).

Without Illich's guts and strength to face loneliness, he could not have avoided the rain dance, gazing into the darkness far enough to discover that we have no future "about which we can say anything, or about which we have any power:" that is "a necessary condition for thinking and reflecting, both with meaningful and sensual words and clear and distinct ideas" (Cayley 1992, 281–282). It is easier to es-cape, to engage in the rain dance.

> Rituals are forms of behavior that make those who participate in them blind to the discrepancy which exists between the purpose for which you perform the rain dance, and the actual social consequences the rain dance has. If the rain dance doesn't work, you can blame yourself for having danced it wrongly. Schooling, I increasingly came to see, is the ritual of a society committed to progress and development. It creates certain myths which are a requirement for a consumer society. For instance, it makes you believe that learning can be sliced up into pieces and quantified, or that learning is something for which you need a process within which you acquire it. And in this process you are the consumer and somebody else the organizer, and you collaborate in pro-ducing the thing which you consume and interiorize (Cayley 1992, 66–67).

The darkness into which Illich has been able to gaze continues pro-ducing human and environmental horrors. More horrifying, perhaps, is the sight of people engaged in every kind of rain dance with frantic breathlessness: packing children off at early dawn into day-care or school confinement; preparing for institutional life—from birth to death hooked to machines; to international institutions, political parties, and

all governments fanatically looking for a good rate of economic growth
to eliminate poverty and injustice; billions of dollars spent on "democratic" elections promoting candidates who will "fix it"; marches and
sit-ins for achieving more satisfaction of *every* possible need . . .

At the grassroots, some people may still be involved in *real* rain
dances: rituals which are part of their tradition. But they know that
they are not buying insurance . . . that they cannot manage or control
the future . . . Without becoming trapped with needs and expectations, they nourish their hopes *(abrigan esperanzas);* keeping them
warm; preventing them from freezing. They know human pain and
suffering cannot be managed (away); they are part of the *conditio
humana.*

The rain dances at the grassroots do not transform the lively present
into an ever-postponed future, a substitute for real hopes and initiatives. The arts of living and dying of common women and men allow
them to deal with the darkness; to dare to see the evil, the horror,
whose shadow emerges as prophets light themselves up as flames in
the darkness. The light that allows us to see is neither the eye nor the
thing it illuminates.

Still, Illich is no role model. For Teodor Shanin and others he is
"the central thinker of our generation." In a review of *Tools for Conviviality,* John Holt stated that

> from now on no analysis that does not include his, extend it, grow out from it,
> can be considered as anything but trivial and misleading (Holt in Hoinacki
> 1996, 4).

Without being anyone's role model, deliberately refusing to be a
media guru, throwing cold water on all brands of Illichisms, Iván Illich
continues to provide incarnated intellectuals the concepts and insights
necessary for taking a critical distance from the dominant modes of
perception; to gaze respectfully at their own differentiated traditions
flourishing in lieu of education (Illich 1973, 1982, 1985, 1987b, 1988,
1989, 1992, 1994c). His radical critique of technological society, and
particularly of the way it shapes our view of reality and generates in
us a set of certainties, is never devoid of hope:

> I have no expectation from technology, but I believe in the beauty, in the
> creativity, in the surprising inventiveness of people, and I continue to hope in
> them (Illich in Cayley 1992, 111).

He believes in "the extraordinary creativity of people and their ability to live in the midst of what frustrates bureaucrats, planners, and

observers" (Cayley 1992, 116). He anticipated an inversion in the structure of tools after a "big, symbolic event." It never happened.

> Instead of that, it is hundreds of millions of people just using their brains and trusting their senses. We now live in a world in which most of those things that industry and government do are misused by people for their own purposes (Illich in Cayley 1992, 117).

Those millions intuitively doing what is needed are increasingly arriving at Illich's insights through common sense; their own as well as that of their own incarnated intellectuals, giving articulation to their resistance transformed into liberation. They have things, models, peers, and elders, as well as reticular structures whose legal, organizational, and technical aspects they try to improve through their daily endeavors (Illich 1970, 109–110).

New technologies and gigantic economic forces are now dismantling the school system, plagued since its creation by every kind of committed reform to establish itself in the stead of peoples' commons. The emerging technological and economic forces conspire to bring to the world more and better education, the universal, multicultural classroom. That they are doomed to fail is irrelevant to the mythmakers, transporting their education rain dance to all corners of the globe.

"Deprived" of their privileges, the peoples of the Two-Thirds World are better able to sense these limits. Bypassing the school, genetic patenting, the Web, biocratic controls, and other horrors of the educated, they are learning from and teaching each other how to mock the economic credo and its disabling goods, services, and professions. Their grassroots epic is evolving with each step they take to return from the future—promised by parties, governments, churches, and all the ideologies of the educated. They are now increasingly aware that the educational system—starting with the school—was the first industrial enterprise that recognized no frontiers; the first "global" corporation, pioneering the reorganization of society to concentrate more and more "labor power" in the creation of consumption "needs" that only highly capitalized corporations can satisfy. Awareness and understanding of this paves the way for alternatives to education, simultaneously attending to the other economic and political structures of society (Illich in Lüning 1974, 21–22). Conviviality is not a futuristic utopia, but part of our present:

> Convivial actualization of the present has taken the place of a future alienated by ideologies . . . Paul Goodman's "reconquest of the present" is brought

about by conviviality. Iván Illich's ideas have introduced a new quality of our human life together into the present (Steger 1984, 300).

Courageously walking their simple, modest, joyful paths, common men and women at the grassroots offer hope to those who desire to escape the traps of colonization, progress, development, and education.

This book is but a fleeting glimpse into their ventures and adventures.

Notes

1   The brilliance of a Chinua Achebe (1961, 1985) reveals these horrors in ways that put them in their proper perspective—particularly in comparison with the scale and virulence of the large-scale horrors that come with colonialism or the neocolonialism of the technological system (Ellul 1964, 1980).

2   For a detailed account of the trapping web of concepts constituting the development discourse, see Sachs 1992.

3   The word has not yet been contaminated or made toxic. For a radical critique of its contemporary use, see "The Mask of Love" in Cayley 1992, 199–218.

4   Reporting on Iván Illich's Spanish reputation, Andoni Alonso takes us back to the 1970s in Spain: "What was at stake was a new way of dealing with education, completely opposed to the patronizing and repressive educational system created by the regime of Generalisimo Francisco Franco." Illich was a crucial influence for that purpose: translating and publishing his works defined an attempt "to develop an entire cultural project opposed to the conservative mediocrity of official thinkers." But in the 1980s, "general interest in Illich temporarily waned . . . In many ways, socialist technocracy was no more than an extension of Franco's program of techno-economic development, but with a democratic facade . . . Most intellectuals now remember Illich's work as exclusively related to pedagogical reform . . . at the exclusion of any real appreciation of his broader and deeper concerns" (Alonso 1996, 243–44). For Alonso, the Spanish image of Ivan Illich can be seen by his English readers as in "a distant mirror" (Alonso 1996, 245). In the mirror offered by Alonso's Spanish Iván Illich, we discern his successes as well as failures in all other schooled, developed societies.

5   See, particularly, Gartner et al. 1973. The book includes articles written as a reaction to Illich's essay, "After Deschooling, What?", published in *Social Policy,* September-October 1971, as well as articles from *Saturday Review* and *Harvard Educational Review.* The book illustrates the academic reaction to Illich's work. For a rigorous account of the reactions to the book, see also: Ohliger and McCarthy 1971, and Ohliger 1974.

6   We eliminated this mistake in our quote offered earlier on in Part II of this book, taken from Illich's *Deschooling Society* (1970, iv–v) which starts with the line: "Universal education through schooling is not feasible." In the edition of *Deschooling Society* we used, the first sentences of this fundamental statement read as follows: "Universal education through schooling is not feasible. It would be more feasible if it were attempted by means of alternative institutions built on the style of present schools." We found it necessary to add a "NOT" in the second sentence. [P.S. After the proofs of our own book were ready, we discovered that other editions of *Deschooling Society* do have a "No" in this very sentence.] Without it, there is a contradiction in the whole

paragraph and with the book; but a contradiction that the readers may refuse to perceive in their search for "alternative institutions built on the style of present schools" as many of them did and still continue to do.

7   "*Scholle*," the word from which school is derived, originally meant leisure.

8   There still abound many Illich critics who argue for the education of the poor, the destitute, or the jobless—claiming schools on their behalf in the name of social justice. The models for such criticism can be found in the many articles written by Herbert Gintis and Vincente Navarro against *Deschooling Society* and *Medical Nemesis*. For Illich's reaction to this pair, see Cayley 1992, 74.

9   For our extended discussion of how the written word—in text, screen, or cyberspace—breaks up commons and communities, creating the atom, the private reader, the individual self with his personal collection of books bought and owned, see Esteva and Prakash, 1997.

10   The argument is now in the media. See the dossier "Reclaiming real life," *Utne Reader*, July-August 1997. Jon Spayde's article, "A way out of wonderland: is a real life possible any more?", starts by stating: "These days I'm hearing the word *real* a lot, mostly from people who have noticed that the demonstrable difference between Bill Clinton and the computer animated spaceman in the movie *Toy Story* is narrowing every day" (49). Ten years ago, finding that Reagan and Mickey Mouse were equally *real* for children was puzzling for many. Spayde's statement is now conventional wisdom.

Epilogue

"Utopia," we understand, refers to "no place" in this world.

What people have been doing in recent years, particularly in the South, we dare to describe as ambiguously utopian: their new eras are already here, offering a pluriverse of alternatives to industrial society. These eras, however, do not yet have *their* marked place. Their grassroots epic of many different tales continues in its marvelous unfolding . . . toward horizons unmanageable, unpredictable.

Rather than globalization, we sense emerging forms of localization; rather than urbanization, ruralization; rather than modernization and individualization, recovery of the present and the commons. If that is what is happening among the social majorities, as we believe, it suggests that ordinary people are using the turbulence of a dying era to go in a thousand different directions; away from the dominant discourse of "a good life," managed and molded by the experts of the establishment.

Following their own sense, they are pioneering some of the most interesting cultural initiatives of our time: those that dare the imagination to go beyond education.

Rooting, Rerooting

The world ceased to be a dream, a prophecy, a project. It has become real. Cultural isolation belongs to the past. There are no peoples, cultures, or societies without "contact" with the "external world": there is interweaving among them. The Web, on a world scale, makes inevitable interactions, interpenetration, interdependence. In such a context, the propensity to unify and homogenize the world has intensified, no longer through ideology but through production: the global farm, the global factory, the global market, the global audience. The new systems of transportation and communication have created a novel sensation of belonging to the world—a form of common existence—captured in the emblem of the global village. Corporative transnationalization, what the experts called internationalization of capital a few decades ago, creates the illusion of full integration, of a deep and complete subsumption of one's being in a globalized reality, confirmed by empirical experience: people across the world using the same brands of jeans or smoking the same brands of cigarettes (or being persuaded by the same campaigns to abandon them). A Mexican soap opera captures record audiences in Russia; an unknown Indian author's story of Kerala gets translated into ten languages and published in seven editions within twelve weeks; gossip about the English royal family reaches Timbuktu and San Francisco in the same second . . .

These descriptors, however, fail to reflect what happens outside the boundaries of the social minorities' world: among those who will never drive a family car; eat in McDonald's; own a mobile or immobile phone; check into a Sheraton . . . It is no longer a secret that the social minorities will have depleted the world's resources well before the contagion of their daily needs overtakes the worlds of the Other. Peoples at the margins have no need to go to school to learn of their increasing *marginalization* from what the minorities are celebrating as the globalized mode of living. They are *experiencing* what the experts call *structural impossibilities*.

Faced with the fact of their exclusion from a way of life proposed as an ideal for everyone, in whose name developers continue sacrificing their environments and commons, the people in *barrios* and villages have started to react. Faced with the globalization of their marginality, they are rooting themselves in spaces which belong to them and to which they belong. To entrench themselves against the forces of uprootedness, they are *localizing* their initiatives and giving them a new meaning: instead of trying to be incorporated into the global promised land, they now claim respect for what they already have; who they are; dedicated to enriching and reclaiming their commons; wrenching them out of the grasp of developers in order to regenerate them, or to try creating new ones.

These trends are overtly manifested among those who have successfully resisted developers' subjugation and avoided being transmogrified into *homines oeconomici* (the possessive individuals born in the West) in their *barrios* and villages. However, they can also be observed among those who were successfully incorporated into the middle classes. The new operation of the transnationalized economy expelled many of them from what they considered their privileges, throwing them into the informal sector. Some of them, like the mass in panic, do crowd themselves at the narrow doors of access to the privileges they lost, joined by aspirants who never knew the condition of institutionalization. Those seeing the reality of the narrow door are walking away, strengthening their joint efforts to cope with their common political and sociological challenges.

Localization or relocalization, taking root again, is being pioneered by those already awake to their marginalization by the global economy.

Ruralization

Urbanization, as a privileged expression of industrial society, imposed a two-pronged dependency: of goods and services necessary for survival and of the mechanisms of access to them. These two prongs—of dependency on the market and the institutions of the welfare state—reshaped the city. The modern city was fragmented into homogeneous and specialized spaces, to accommodate the economic functions defined for the people. To get subsistence out of that logic became virtually impossible.

The process of urbanization has apparently concluded in the industrial societies. Seventy-five percent of its population is urban, while most nonurbanites are assimilated into the same pattern. The invention of the commuter and the search for a better quality of life stopped the growth of cities; while its logic of operation defines more than ever before the daily life of *homo transportandus.*

Urbanization continues in the southern hemisphere, where the urban population is still increasing at a rate of 4 percent a year. Nine out of the ten most populated cities of the world are now in the South. In regions like Latin America, the urban population will soon catch up with and surpass the percentages of industrial countries. The experts predict that the urban population of the world will rise to 60 percent of the total in the year 2000.

Alternative trends are suggested by the *visible* deceleration of urbanization, already observed in many countries. There are also signs of its changing nature. For, till recently, the growth of the city always occurred at the expense of the *barrio.* The diversity and multifunctionality of the latter, tending to self-sufficiency, entered into continual contradiction with the economic logic of urbanization. Whole *barrios* were devastated in order to impose the logic of specialized sectors—for sleeping, working, or buying goods and services, all of them interconnected by speedways needed by urbanites to fulfill their functions.

Those suffering the consequences of this devastation have started to react. Since urbanization in the South has effectively fulfilled its dissolving and destructive function, without providing employment opportunities or urban goods and services, the people have been forced to rely upon themselves for their subsistence. Their rural traditions, still recent, have helped them in "illegal" land takeovers and the organization of their settlements. With ingenuity, they endow themselves, legally or illegally, with the "basic services" that the government will not; building their houses, using their subsistence skills to occupy the interstices of economic society, and thriving within them in their own ways. These include maintaining their organic relationships with the rural communities from which they came, facilitating flows of people and products in both directions.

The economic turbulence of recent years, including the debt crisis, has strengthened and nourished their social fabrics, further stimulating such double trends: to enrich rural settlements through the reformulation of urban techniques, while ruralizing the city, reclaiming and regenerating the multifunctional *barrio,* in all its diversity. In the big urban settlements of the South, modern enclaves, widened to accommodate the middle classes, are literally under siege by the complex social fabric of those they call "street people."

Of necessity, this fabric is inextricably linked to the market of the middle classes; but these street people would be wiped out if they submitted to its abstract logic. They live, eat, find shelter, sing, dance, and celebrate through their millions of informal initiatives for the "ruralization" of the cities.

Reclaiming the Commons

The enclosure of the commons not only tore women and men from their land and their household economy, but also ripped them from the social fabric through which they derived support and comfort. Those who were not absorbed by the factories nor operated as parts of the industrial reserve army were treated as castoffs. Many of them were forced to emigrate.

In the countries of the southern hemisphere, the enclosure followed a different pattern. When it did not enslave the people, it subordinated them to the requirements of colonialism, exploiting them without expelling them from their commons. When the expulsion was pushed forward through methods like the Green Revolution, the capacity to employ the people was always very limited and great numbers of people were left behind. There were constant resettlements of people, but many of them had no place to emigrate. Since they could no longer function as functionaries of the industrial reserve army, they became disposable human beings.

They naturally reacted—often staying alive by the skin of their teeth. Those who could, resisted colonialists and developers, concentrating their efforts on the regeneration of their traditional places and commons. Many others, who lost their traditional commons, struggled to reclaim them in the countryside; or they created new ones in the city. They did not attempt to *come back* to the condition they had before colonization or development: an obvious impossibility. They rooted their efforts to improve their differentiated ways of life in their traditions; without any longer being able to assume or to understand them as a destiny. Their traditions prevented them from falling under the industrial ethos, with its arrogant presence of controlling the future. They avoided the expectations which come with the assumption of scarcity or of the individual self.

Individualization, one element in the modern logic, reduces people to the minimal unit of several abstract categories. The individual is a passenger—in a flight, a client or professional, a student or professor—in the economic society; a housewife or a family head, in its sexist regime; a citizen or a foreigner in the nation-state. Those individualized in the abstract category of castoffs, the unemployable, cannot but find their condition to be unbearable. In contrast, however, from those educated from birth to be individuals, those robbed of their communal polity *(comunalidad)* have it in their flesh. They have within them the capacities and skills for regenerating and enriching their spaces—not as some futurist utopia but as a part of the present being actualized; free of the baggage of alienated and alienating ideologies about the individual self. They know that, instead of being individuals, they are *personal knots in nets of relationships:* the nets have given them a place to which they belong and which belongs to them.

David and Goliath

Global forces, operating today under the banners of free trade and other neoliberalisms, are mortal swells weakening nation-states. Their privileged incumbents search for security and control within ever bigger macrostructures, expecting to soften and moderate the blind forces of the market.

Rather than following such impulses, increasingly incapable of holding back the oceanic force of the new economic storms, peoples rooted in their commons search for the autonomy that comes with the human scale of their political bodies. To protect them from being drowned or swallowed up, their grassroots initiatives build dikes to contain these global forces to their margins.

Every struggle of autonomy demonstrates that these global forces can only have concrete existence in their local incarnations. In that territory of their commons, David always has the possibility of winning over Goliath. And the emerging coalitions of well-rooted women and men, at the grassroots, are articulating their local advances, formulating and enacting the political controls required to protect and strengthen their ventures.

Every day offers new documentation about the successes of the people in such endeavors, obtained after hard and long struggles. Their failures or new threats are also documented. They confront severe restrictions and it would be criminal to idealize the misery in which many of them live. They harbor no illusions of an ideal life.

They live their ideals every day. Their epic unfolds outside the brutal, vicious grasp of global forces. They continue to share the humble hope that Pandora did not let escape from her amphora. In their shifting horizon, their institutional inversions reveal the brilliant and diffuse colors of the rainbow.

References

Achebe, C. (1961). No longer at ease (reprint). London: Heinemann.

―――. (1985). Things fall apart (reprint). London: Heinemann.

Alamán, L. (1985). Historia de México desde los primeros movimientos que prepararon su independencia en el año de 1808 hasta la época presente. México: Fondo de Cultura Económica.

Alonso, A. (1996). A Spanish Ivan Illich. Bulletin of Science, Technology and Society 16 (5&6), 243–245.

Apffel Marglin, F. (1995, November 27). Personal communication to Gustavo Esteva.

―――. (Ed. with Proyecto Andino de Tecnologias Campesinas; Andean Project of Peasant Technologies). (forthcoming). Production or regeneration? An Andean perspective on modern western knowledge. London: Zed Books.

Arévalo, L. (1992, August 21). Interview, partially published as: Renovar las raíces. Opciones 16, 9–10.

Ariès, P. (1962). Centuries of childhood: A social history of family life. New York: Vintage.

Autonomedia. (1994). Zapatistas! Documents of the new Mexican revolution. New York: Autonomedia.

Berger, J. (1991). And our faces, my heart, brief as photos. New York: Vintage.

Berry, W. (1972). A continuous harmony: Essays cultural and agricultural. New York: Harcourt, Brace, Jovanovich.

————. (1977). The unsettling of America: Culture and agriculture. San Francisco: Sierra Club.

————. (1983). Standing by words. San Francisco: North Point Press.

————. (1987). Home economics. San Francisco: North Point Press.

————. (1990). What are people for? San Francisco: North Point Press.

————. (1991a, February). Out of your car, off your horse. Atlantic Monthly, 61–63.

————. (1991b, Winter). Nobody loves this planet. In Context, 27, 4.

————. (1992). Sex, economy, freedom, and community. San Francisco: Pantheon.

Bhabha, H. K. (1994). The location of culture. New York: Routledge.

————. (1997, Winter). Life at the border: Hybrid identities of the present. New Perspectives Quarterly 14 (1), 30–31.

Bonfil, G. (1996). México profundo: Reclaiming a civilization. Austin: University of Texas Press.

Braverman, H. (1975). Labor and monopoly capital: The degradation of work in the twentieth century. New York: Monthly Review Press.

Caffentzis, C. G. (1997, Spring). The international intellectual property regime and the enclosure of African knowledge. Committee for Academic Freedom in Africa. Newsletter, 1, 14–19.

Cárdenas, L. (1978). Speech in Tepecoacuilco, Gro. April 17, 1937. Palabras y documentos públicos de Lázaro Cárdenas—1928/ 1940. México: Siglo XXI, 242.

Cardoso de Oliveira, R. 1990. Prácticas interétnicas y moralidad. Por un indigenismo (auto)crítico. América Indígena I (4), 9–25.

Cayley, D. (1992). Ivan Illich in conversation. Concord: House of Anansi Press.

Clastres, P. (1987). Society against the state: Essays in political anthropology. New York: Zone Books.

CNCSRFCRS (Comisión Nacional para la Conmemoración del Sesquicentenario de la República Federal y el Centenario de la Restauración del Senado). (1974). Presentación. Acta Constitutiva de la Federación. México.

Cougar, Y. (1973). Review of Discovery of the individual, by C. Morris. Revue des Sciences Philosophiques et Theologiques 57, 305–7.

Dag Hammarskjold Foundation. (1975). What now? Another development. Development Dialogue. Uppsala: Dag Hammarskjold Foundation.

Dewey, J. (1962). Individualism old and new. New York: Capricorn.

————. (1963). Experience and education. New York: Collier.

Díaz, F. (1992, April). Interview, partially published as: En el reino de los deberes. Opciones 19, 10–11.

Dumont, L. (1977). From Mandeville to Marx: Genesis and triumph of economic ideology. Chicago: University of Chicago Press.

Ecologist, The. (1993). Whose common future?: Reclaiming the commons. Philadelphia: New Society Publishers.

Ellul, J. (1964). The technological society. New York: Knopf.

————. (1980). The technological system. New York: Continuum.

Esteva, G. (1980). Economía y enajenación. México: Universidad Veracruzana.

————. (1987, January). Regenerating people's space. Alternatives XII-1, 125–152.

————. (1991). Muerte y transfiguración de la ciudad de México. México: Opción.

————. (1992). Fiesta—jenseits von entwicklung, hilfe und politik. Frankfurt: Brandes & Apsel/Südwind.

————. (1993, Spring). A new source of hope: The margins. Interculture XXVI (2), 119, 2–62.

————. (1994a, May/June). Basta! Mexican Indians say 'enough.' The Ecologist 24 (3), 83–84.

————. (1994b). Crónica del fin de una era. México: Posada.

Esteva, G., & Prakash, M. S. (1992). Resistance to sustainable development: Lessons from the banks of the Narmada. The Ecologist 22 (2), 45–51.

————. (1996, Summer/Fall). Grassroots postmodernism. Interculture XXIX (2), 3–52.

————. (1997). Grassroots postmodernism: Remaking the Soil of Cultures. London: Zed Books.

Falbel, A. (1993, May/June). Learning? Yes of course. Education? No thanks. Growing Without Schooling 92, 13–14.

Falquet, F. L. (1995). La violencia cultural del sistema educativo: Las mujeres indígenas víctimas de la escuela. San Cristóbal de Las Casas: Instituto de Asesoría Antropológica de la Región Maya. Doc. 044-V-95.

Foucault, M. (1977). Power/knowledge. New York: Pantheon.

————. (1983). Preface (xi–xiv). Deleuze, G., & Guattari, F. Anti-oedipus: Capitalism and schizophreniaMinneapolis: University of Minnesota Press.

Freire, P. (1993). Pedagogy of the oppressed. New York: Continuum.

Gandhi, M. K. (1953). Hind Swaraj or Indian home rule. Ahmedabad: Navajivan Press.

————. (1953). Towards new education. Ahmedabad: Navajivan Press.

————. (1970). Essential writings. Selected and edited by V.V. Ramana Murti. New Delhi: Gandhi Peace Foundation.

Gartner, A., Greer, C., & Riessman, F. (Eds.). (1973). After deschooling, what? New York: Harper & Row.

Gilly, A., Subcomandante Marcos, & Ginzburg, C. (1995). Discusión sobre la historia. México: Aguilar, Altea, Taurus, Alfaguara. The interview with Subcomandante Marcos was celebrated by Carmen Castillo and Tessa Brisac in Aguascalientes, Chiapas, October 24, 1994.

Girard, R. (1978). To double business bound: Essays on literature, mimesis and anthropology. Baltimore: Johns Hopkins Press.

González y González, L. (1974). El periodo formativo. In Historia mínima de México, Cosío D. et al. México: El Colegio de México.

Goodman, P. (1962). Compulsory miseducation and the community of scholars. New York: Vintage.

———. (1969). New reformation: Notes of a neolithic conservative. New York: Vintage.

———. (1977). Drawing the line: Political essays. Ed. by Taylor Stoehr. New York: Free Life.

Gordon, A., & Newfield, C. (Eds.). (1996). Mapping multiculturalism. Minneapolis: University of Minnesota Press.

Green, T. (1980). Predicting the behavior of the educational system. Syracuse: Syracuse University Press.

Groeneveld, S., Hoinacki, L., Illich, I., and friends. (1991). The earthy virtue of place. New Perspectives Quarterly 8 (1), 59.

Growing Without Schooling. Cambridge, Massachusetts: Holt Associates.

Guehenno, J. M. (1995). The end of the nation-state. Minnesota: University of Minnesota Press.

Havel, V. (1985). The power of the powerless. Armonk, New York: M. E. Sharpe.

Heath, S. B. (1972). La política del lenguaje en México. De la colonia a la nación. México: Secretaría de Educación Pública/Instituto Nacional de Educación de Adultos.

Henry, J. (1963). Culture against man. New York: Random House.

———. (1971). The vulnerability in education. Essays on education. Harmondsworth, England: Penguin Books.

Hern, M. (Ed.). (1996). Deschooling our lives. Philadelphia: New Society.

Hoinacki, L. (1996). Ivan Illich—A view of his work. Science, Technology and Society Program, Pennsylvania State University. Typs.

Holt, J. (1965). How children fail. New York: Pitman.

———. (1972). Freedom and beyond. New York: Dutton.

———. (1974). Escape from childhood. New York: Dutton.

———. (1976). Instead of education. New York: Dutton.

Ignatieff, M. (1984). The needs of strangers. New York: Viking.

Illich, I. (1970). Deschooling society. New York: Harper & Row.

———. (1971a). Celebration of awareness: A call for institutional revolution. London: Marion Boyers.

———. (1971b). On the necessity to deschool society. CIDOC Doc. I/V. 71/3.

———. (1973). Tools for conviviality. New York: Harper & Row.

———. (1974a). After deschooling, what?. London: Writers and Readers Publishing Cooperative.

———. (1974b). En América Latina, ¿para qué sirve la escuela?. Buenos Aires: Ediciones Búsqueda.

———. (1977). Towards a history of needs. Berkeley: Heyday Books.

———. (1981). Shadow work. London: Marion Boyars.

———. (1982). Gender. New York: Pantheon.

———. (1985). H_2O and the waters of forgetfulness. Berkeley: Heyday Books.

———. (1987a). La alfabetización de la mentalidad. Un llamamiento a investigarla. Tecnopolítica 87, 04, 1–9.

———. (1987b). Hospitality and pain. Science, Technology and Society Program, Pennsylvania State University. Typs.

———. (1988). Computer literacy and the cybernetic dream. Science, Technology and Society Program, Pennsylvania State University. Typs.

———. (1989, Spring). The shadow our future throws. New Perspectives Quarterly 6 (1), 20–24.

———. (1992). In the mirror of the past. London: Marion Boyars.

———. (1993). In the vineyard of the text. Chicago: University of Chicago Press.

————. (1994a). An address to Master Jacques. Bulletin of Science, Technology and Society 14 (2), 65–68.

————. (1994b). Guarding the eye in the age of show. Science, Technology and Society Program, Pennsylvania State University. Typs.

————. (1994c). Blasphemy: A radical critique of technological culture. Science, Technology and Society Program, Pennsylvania State University. Typs.

————. (1996). Education in the perspective of the dropout. Bulletin of Science, Technology and Society 16 (5–6), 257–261.

————. (1997, Winter). From fast to quick. New Perspectives Quarterly, 14 (1), 12.

Illich, I., Kenneth, I., et al. (1977). Disabling professions. New York: Marion Boyars.

Illich, I., & Rieger, M. (1996). The wisdom of Leopold Kohr. Science, Technology and Society Program, Pennsylvania State University. Typs.

International Conference on Rethinking Human Rights. (1994, December). Just world trust. Kuala Lumpur, Malaysia.

Janeway, E. (1980). Powers of the weak. New York: Alfred A. Knopf.

Kohr, L. (1992). Size cycles. Fourth World Review 54, 10–11.

Kumar, S. (Ed.). (1980). The Schumacher lectures. New York: Harper.

Lao Tzu (1997). Tao te ching (Gia-fu Feng and Jane English, Trans.). New York: Vintage Books.

Lauderdale, P. (1991). Indigenous North American alternatives to modern law and punishment: Lessons of nature. Science, Technology and Society Program, Pennsylvania State University. Typs.

Leonard, G. (1992, May). The end of school. The Atlantic Monthly, 24–32.

Loyo, E. (1985). El cardenismo y la educación de adultos. In Historia de la alfabetización y de la educación de adultos en México, Seminario de Historia de la Educación, El Colegio de México. México: Secretaría de Educación Pública/Instituto Nacional de Educación de Adultos.

Lummis, D. (1996). Radical democracy. Ithaca: Cornell University Press.

Lüning, H. (Ed.). (1974). La escuela y la represión de nuestros hijos. Madrid: Sociedad de Educación Atenas.

MacIntyre, A. (1981). After virtue. Notre Dame: University of Notre Dame Press.

Maldonado, B. (1988, December). La escuela indígena como camino hacia la ignorancia. Paper presented at the Second Reunion for the exchange of Educational Experiences in the Indigenous Environment, Oaxaca de Juárez, México.

Martínez, L. J. (1992, November 27). Interview, partially published as: Fabricar la propia vida. Opciones 23, 11–13.

Meadows, D. H. (and others). (1972). The limits to growth. New York: New American Library.

Menchú, R. (1994). I, Rigoberta Menchú—An Indian woman in Guatemala. New York: Verso.

Molloy, D. (1991, February 1). Education: Time to act. The Aisling Magazine, 17–22.

Nandy, A. (1981). The intimate enemy. Loss and recovery of self under colonialism. New York: Oxford University Press.

———. (1996). Gandhi after Gandhi. Centre for the Study of Developing Societies. Typs.

Ohliger, J. (1974). Bibliography of comments on the Illich-Reimer deschooling theses. Educational Resource Clearinghouse ED 090 145.

Ohliger, J., & McCarthy, C. (1971). Lifelong learning or lifelong schooling? A tentative view of the ideas of Ivan Illich with a quotational bibliography. Syracuse, N.Y.: Syracuse University Publications in Continuing Education.

Orr, D. (1992). Ecological literacy: Education and the transition to a postmodern world. Albany: SUNY Press.

Panikkar, R. (1978). Myth, faith and hermeneutics. New York: Paulist Press.

————. (1990). The pluralism of truth. In World Faiths Insight. New Series 26, 1–16.

————. (1993). La diversidad como presupuesto para la armonía entre los pueblos. Wisay Marka (Barcelona) 20, 15–20.

————. (1995). Invisible harmony. Minneapolis: Fortress Press.

Paz, O. (1996, June). Agravio y desagravio. Vuelta 235, 67.

Polanyi, K. (1975). The great transformation. New York: Octagon Books. (Reprinted from The great transformation, K. Polanyi, 1944, New York: Rinehart.)

Pörksen, U. (1995). Plastic words. University Park, PA: Pennsylvania State University Press.

Postman, N. (1996). The end of education. New York: Vintage.

Prakash, M. S. (1993, Autumn). Gandhi's postmodern education: Ecology, peace, and multiculturalism relinked. Wholistic Education Review 6 (3), 8–17.

————. (1994). What are people for? Wendell Berry on Education, Ecology and Culture. Educational Theory 44 (2), 135–157.

Robert, J. (1996). Trust people. Mexico: Habitat International Coalition.

Sachs, W. (Ed.). (1992). The development dictionary: A guide to knowledge as power. London: Zed.

————. (1997, Winter). Wasting time is an ecological virtue. New Perspectives Quarterly 14 (1), 4–10.

Sahagún, Fray Bernardino de. (1986). Coloquios y doctrina cristiana con que los doce frailes de San Francisco, enviados por el Papa Adriano VI y por el emperador Carlos V, convirtieron a los indios de la Nueva España. Reprinted in Los diálogos de 1524 según el texto de Fray Bernardino de Sahagún y sus colaboradores indígenas, Ed. by León Portilla, M. México: UNAM.

Sahlins, M. (1972). Stone age economics. New York: Aldine.

Sandoval, F., & Sandoval, M. (1992, May). Interview, partially published as: La Casa Que Recoge Nuestro Camino (The house that collects our path.) Opciones, 4, 8–10.

Sen, A. (1981). Poverty & famines: An essay on entitlement & deprivation. Oxford: Oxford University Press.

Schwartz, D. (1997). Who cares? Re-discovering community. Boulder: Westview Press.

Steger, H. (1984). Conviviality. In H. Steger (Ed.), Alternatives in Education. Munich: Wilhelm Fink Werlag München.

Streeten, P. (1979). A basic needs approach to economic development. In Jameson, K.P. & Kilber, C.K. (Eds.) Directions in Economic Development. Notre Dame: University of Notre Dame Press.

Toffler, A. (1992, May 19). ¿Cuáles son los nuevos poderes?. El Nacional. Taken from Actuel, 3.

Truman, H. S. (1949, January 20). Inaugural Address. Documents on American Foreign Relations. Connecticut: Princeton University Press.

Vachon, R. (1990). L'étude du pluralisme juridique—une approche diatopique et dialogale. Journal of Legal Pluralism and Unofficial Law 29, 163–173.

———. (1991). Human rights and dharma. Montreal: Intercultural Institute of Montreal. Typs.

———. (1991/1992). The Mohawk nation and its communities. Interculture XXIV & XV (4 & 1), 1–35, 1–25.

———. (1995a, Spring, Summer, Fall). Guswenta or the intercultural imperative. Interculture XXVII, 2,3,4, (127, 128, 129), 1–73, 98–111, 146–171.

———. (1995b, Summer). From global perspective to an open horizon, an ever deepening synthesis. Holistic Education Review, 54–56.

Vora, R. (1993, July/September). Gandhi's so-called inconsistencies: An analysis with referrence to nonviolence, reason, and faith. Gandhi Marg, 137–154.

Wolf, E. (1958). La formación de la nación: un ensayo de formulación. Ciencias Sociales (Washington) IV 20/21/22, 50–62.

Index